Alive
in God's World

By the Same Author

So That You May be One
(Lindisfarne Books, 1997)

Alive
in God's World

Human Life on Earth
and in Heaven
As Described in

THE VISIONS OF
JOA BOLENDAS

Compiled, Translated, and Introduced by John Hill

Foreword by Therese Schroeder-Sheker

LINDISFARNE BOOKS

Published by Lindisfarne Books
P.O. Box 799
Great Barrington, MA 01230

The major part of this work was published as *Die Schöpfung Mensch: Nach Visionen von Joa Bolendas,* copyright © 1999 Jom Verlag, Switzerland.

Library of Congress Cataloging-in-Publication Data

Bolendas, Joa.
    [Schöpfung Mensch. English]
    Alive in God's world: human life on earth and in heaven as described in the visions of Joa Bolendas / compiled, translated, and introduced by John Hill; foreword by Therese Schroeder-Sheker.
        p. cm.
    Includes bibliographical references (p.).
    ISBN 0-9701097-5-X
    1. Bolendas, Joa. 2. Mystics – Switzerland – Biography. 3. Private revelations.
    4. Spiritual life. I. Hill, John, 1943- II. Title.

BV5095.B75 A3 2001
248.2'9 – dc21

                                                                          2001020235

Designed by ediType
10 9 8 7 6 5 4 3 2 1

Printed in the United States of America

Contents

Part Two
ALIVE IN HEAVEN:
RISEN FROM THE DEAD

The Risen Ones Speak

– Foreword –

Steered by Grace—
The Mystical Life of Joa Bolendas

by Therese Schroeder-Sheker

Gather up the fragments... that nothing may be lost.
—John 6:12

What an honor, responsibility, and challenge it is to champion anything freely given or truly new. Everyone has to risk, to trust different ways of knowing, to feel forward into possibility, and to be willing to enter into the unknown. The works of the Swiss mystic Joa Bolendas (b. 1917) are just that, *new*, and freely given from heaven to earth. The people who have worked on this book have been filled with a multitude of varied experiences precisely because *Alive in God's World* is a living legacy. The editorial team is anxious to make Joa's charism further known to the world, and in this essay, I'm going to try to gather up some scattered fragments and forgotten details in order to weave the various currents into a fabric that might serve several purposes. In doing so, I understand it to be of value to describe some of the unique elements that have been part and parcel of this endeavor over the years. These are the ones that may give future readers deeper insight into the mystical life of Joa Bolendas, as well as of the transmission process involved for the compilers and editors.

A forest of normal and at times chaotic obstacles occur in any new endeavor. To do something truly new, people of good will are also called to clear away the wild impassioned underbrush of soul; to haul away by the sweat of the brow granite boulders of thought, religious, personal and cultural conditioning; to mend each broken spirit wheel that no longer turns, returns, or carries; and then, beyond ourselves, to face the gales and tempests of life itself. These elements can make individuals or groups hesitant or doubtful, or worse yet, be tempted into diagnosing the obstacles as ominous signs rather than part of the assignment as well as of God's story and glory. Then too, aside from our own strengths or limitations, there are still the qualities of soil, sunlight, rain, and wind that make or break the sweetness in the fruit harvested from the heavenly orchard. It's all beyond personal effort or control. Preparing a living book about the mystical life from any time period resembles the work of the gardener who stewards that same orchard on the side of God's hill close to the New Jerusalem. Publishing the mystical works of one who is still very much alive poses different kinds of opportunities and conditions from those initiatives in which the legacy is made available posthumously. The visions and spirit conversations of Joa Bolendas are golden apples of the sun, and gathering them into bouquets for healing, praise, and service asks for particular kinds of readiness and wakefulness. Please allow me to make this less abstract.

How many of us have longed to be able to walk alongside Francis of Assisi (ca. 1182–1226), hear him sing his "Canticle of the Sun," change his bandaged eyes after they were cauterized, or to be near him after the Seraph came with the stigmata in September? To be able to learn from him how to integrate intense suffering and joy, lyricism and purity? Who would not long to ask Mechthild of Hackeborn (1241–1298 or 1299) about the harp issuing from the heart of Christ, or about the quality of His voice when He sang His love, the sound of his heartbeats, or the whirling discs in Mary's robe? To allow oneself to be changed and reorganized by the ineffable, and then to let go and cherish rather then possess? Who would not want to visit the forest monk Seraphim of Sarov (1759–1833) whose face shone like the sun, who took the whole world into his heart, and oh, to be able to ask him advice about certain kinds of purgation, the geography of prolonged silence, intimacy with Mary, and the discernment of spirits. I cite these exemplars from earlier periods in order to make a point about the process available to us today in working with the legacy of Joa Bolendas.

While one can pray and meditate on Francis, Mechthild, or

Seraphim, and *we do,* that kind of interior soul converse is different from the sustained dialogue in time and space that can occur now with Joa, a Swiss woman in her mid-eighties. Fifty or two hundred years from now, musicologists, seekers, or historians of spirituality won't have to find her diaries or *visionlieder* and wonder what the corpus is. Hopefully, those readers will continue to ask penetrating questions, uncover far more than we have, and with certitude, they will have wished that any number of people on our team had asked her perhaps better questions, but these seekers won't be entirely in the dark. For several decades, a very small group of people has been able to go to her with questions, been able to ask her to elaborate on the visions, the hymns, the beings, the symbols, the virtues, and more. To further ground the picture, imagine a scene from real life. Can you sense what it is like to sit in the privacy of Joa's room and sing and play the harp for her? Imagine the humility and privilege to be told without reservation: "Yes, *yes* ... that's it ... reverence ... the angels sing it *this* way ... yes ... hands open ... here, a swelling ... there ... pianissimo ... " Among other things, she describes heavenly pitch differently than terrestrial pitch, and so you see, provides us with direct contact, inspiration and substance.

Imagine, too, being the translator John Hill, her junior by a generation, yet her partner in prayer and the one who has sustained many questions, struggles, and an ever-deepening sense of wonder. I asked him once what he had personally learned from Joa during these decades, and he said in a moment of crystal clear recollection, "She has taught me how to pray, to fight, and to love." Everything about this preface, then, is an attempt to portray some of the creativity, complexity, ardor and nuance that has characterized the two major English-translation publication efforts on Joa Bolendas. I'll start in the very present as a point of departure, and then backtrack chronologically.

Right Here and Now: God's World!

This second volume is a companion to the first volume on Joa's work, entitled *So That You May Be One.* During three years with the new work, I have slipped on the title a number of times, and even now, still occasionally register the name of this endeavor as "Alive in God's *Word.*" A sweet slip, not a hard fall. But by the presence or absence of a single consonant, one is inadvertently handed a golden key and thus spiritual entrée to the work.

As readers new to Joa Bolendas are about to discover, Joa is alive and thriving in God's word. She has the ear of the heart, and allows it to steer her in grace. It is that fact that has fostered her prayerful capacity to be equally alive in God's *word* or alive in God's *world.* The Logos is generative, and from this mystery, all of Creation comes into being. The basis of Joa's spirituality is the commitment to daily prayer, to pray in new and living ways, to read the Bible faithfully, to embody it. She takes the Logos into the very fabric of her life—body, soul, and spirit. She puts time aside, reserved wholly for listening to this Logos. She sees and she hears; she enters into deep conversation and communion with Christ. She responds to the world that has opened itself up to her at as many levels as are possible, given her station in life. She has said "yes," over and over, during forty-four years, to change, to meet the seemingly impossible, to make herself available to become malleable. She allows herself to be conformed to God's will, to bow in the face of His requests, as well as those of Mary, the saints and angels. She brings questions, struggles, and sings praise. Like Jacob, she has at times wrestled all night with the angel.

What about God's world? What are we talking about? What has this to do with the world in which we live? What preparation or formation occurred in the life of Joa Bolendas, a woman of the twentieth century, that fostered this grace? She didn't lead the life of a Mechthild in a cloister. What was Joa's golden key?

Throughout history, readers from every walk of life who either approach or stumble across the Book of Books share a common bond. We find that reading and digesting the Bible is a radical activity. It is a quickener. It costs us too! It's not possible to read it and remain the same. It shakes the very world of the reader upside down and topples the stratified Jericho of any walled-in human heart. It is not possible to read God's word without it sparking an inner revolution, one that asks us to stretch and to grow, turn and return, grapple and surrender, praise and question. In God's word, we enter God's world and God's way. It is not the same world or way as Man's, but it could be, one day.

Continued prayerful daily reading of the sacred texts (or even desperate and sporadic thumbing of them) asks readers for everything and, somehow, for "nothing"—no thing. When reading the scriptures, we are asked to sustain perennial problems and eternal mysteries, asked to sustain confusing paradoxes and troubling enigmas, contradictory narratives and subtle indications, soul heat and spirit longing, wilderness and paradise—*simultaneously!* At a certain point, such inner work abandons that beguiling demand for explanations. Yet in their place, in the place where there is sometimes "nothing," we receive new capacities. Reading the word of God always carves us out, makes us more, makes the reception of God's response possible in an ever-deepening current of love and power. Joa didn't have a Damascus experience. Rather, she allowed herself to be quickened by the word of God and especially by the New Testament. In a secular era when this is scorned, she is a disciple of Jesus Christ, and a Christian in the truest, most personally demanding, and deepest sense.

So That You May Be One: A Retrospective Gaze

The comprehensive volume that first introduced Joa Bolendas to the English speaking world is titled *So That You May Be One* (Lindisfarne Press, 1997). This edition of her visions "merely" excerpts entries from forty years of journals and inner work, all of which are painstakingly translated by John Hill, an Irishman living and working in Zurich. The first volume is almost entirely reserved for visions, with very sparse commentary. This overall work reflects Joa's life as a mystic, a contemplative active in the world in that she is connected to family and community, yet choosing to remain hidden from publicity. She writes under a pseudonym so that no attention is drawn to her personhood. As a Protestant, the visions Joa experienced were anything but sought. The visions came about as the direct fruit of prayer and systematic Biblical readings from both the Hebrew Scriptures and the New Testament, coupled with the events of her life as a mother and a wife living in a small mountain village. Joa was the supportive spouse of a parson in the Swiss Reformed Church. She was active in her congregation. Her life includes joy and tragedy. She integrated God's word and way into the fullness of her life. Throughout all, she pondered the words of the Living Book, prayed over and with them, questioned and loved them, let them reorganize her and bless her, quicken her and unsettle her, and by extension, everyone who came into contact with her! Through the living word, she directly entered God's world. In the visions, she is largely approached by Jesus, Mary, the Evangelists, a few particular saints, some angels, and the souls of a very few people who have recently died.

This first volume also provided a bilingual section devoted to the mystical hymns or *visionlieder*. The Swiss-Canadian (and bilingual) Miriam Mason, who has sung these hymns all her life, provided the world with sensitive English renderings. Additionally, we included transcriptions of a dozen of the *visionlieder* which Joa received directly from angels, saints, and Risen Ones during the course of the decades. There are no human filters or overlays in these simple transcriptions, such as will come later with beautiful and startling piano, orchestral, and choral arrangements submitted by prayerful composers like the devoted Austrian artist Peter Barcaba, or the deceased pianist Franz Eibner. Joa heard a mystical chorus of angels singing—sometimes these singers came solo—and thus provided us with a kind of music that is a genuine renewal of hymnody as well as a kind of medicine for different ailments of body, soul, or spirit or their combinations. At the Chalice of Repose Project, we too have not only employed the *visionlieder* at the bedside of those gravely ill, but have also arranged for concert settings of several pieces in new ways, emphasizing the Johannine message, God's indwelling and ever brightening light, by combining three-part harmony *a cappella* voices with layers of bells, so that the light is increasingly scintillating and shimmering. At other times, for vigils and for concerts, we have made harp arrangements, drawing low deep tones from the bass strings, while relying heavily on the uses of harmonics in the treble for all the same reasons. However, the world needs the original unfiltered hymns, unadorned, and this is what *So That You May Be One* provides.

Also critical to *So That You May Be One* is the accompanying essay by Dr. Robert Sardello ("The Visions of Joa Bolendas: An Introduction") in which he addresses the nature of revelation and inspiration from the discipline and insight of spiritual psychology. Here, he differentiates vision material, received in wide awake consciousness, from the work of "channels" or mediums who speak from a variety of psychic levels, and often from a state in which they retain no memory. In other words, they lose consciousness. He further differentiates between information and transformation, makes observations about the manner in which Joa's visions occurred, different ways of knowing, the role of faith in higher ways of knowing, and inner and outer unity, individual and between the Christian churches.

Additionally, for the first volume, the spiritual amanuensis John Hill wrote an important foreword describing the translating process, Joa's theology, the role his Jungian formation might play on the way in which he lived and worked with the visions, and the nature of Joa's message—the dual effects of faith and experience and the importance of hope. Joa's work might not ever have been made available had John not literally made a commitment decades ago to rearrange his life to meet and sit and pray with her week after week, year after year. His creative contribution could not be overestimated; it has been, among other things, one of faithfulness, insight, collaboration, question, dialogue, and *participatory* prayer. His translations faithfully resist abstraction.

I too wrote in depth ("I Heard the Call of the Seraph") about the alchemy of sung prayer, transubstantiation in the Mass and in prayer, about the *visionlieder*, the musical content of the visions, and the spirituality of listening which is so central to the entire tradition of prayer in Jewish and Christian worlds. As a concert and recording artist, musician-clinician, and scholar of the women mystics, I was asked by the publishers for something slightly more than straightforward musicology. So it is that I described something of the nature of my own encounter and relationship with this mystic and her *visionlieder* during a decade from the 1980s to the 1990s. I tried to hint at the possibility of a way of singing from the future that encompasses transubstantiation.

The Narrative of Gratitude

In rounding off this picture about the first volume, it seems timely to let readers know *how* the publication actually came into being, that is to say, how it moved from diary to manuscript to book available to the world at large. I have already alluded to the weekly listening-responding prayer process that Joa and John have lived for many years. From this, readers can only imagine the efforts John and editors have made not only in selecting entries but in the translations. When the first volume became fairly formed, that is to say, translated by John, chosen, collated, and formed in another private notebook, aching to be shared with a new world of readers, the Americans surfaced.

The details of our personal lives mean little, but the ways in which people are personally affected by the presence of God in daily life is critical. For this reason, we bring a few very human details to light, although they are transpersonal details. When people discovered Joa's work, the visions or the *visionlieder*, they had true encounters. It is the depth of the experience that calls people into action and verifies the validity of their decisions and impressions. The following anecdotes and facts serve to remember and acknowledge how many people allowed themselves to be steered by grace, some of whom are already in heaven.

I had first encountered Joa spiritually through her Christmas angel some eighteen months prior to meeting her. My first actual meeting with Joa occurred on an initial visit made possible through the support of a Dutch woman named Gidi Croes. Gidi is a kind of spiritual grandmother to a number of people; she is one of the many Dutch people who lived to tell the story of World War II, and of her survival living hidden in between two walls during the time of the Nazi occupation. She knows what it is to be forced to trust your instincts and to rely on them wholeheartedly. At an early age, she developed other ways of knowing. For many years, Joa had refrained from receiving strangers and unknown visitors. She received family members and friends of family. After having sought her out and verified that we would be received, Gidi and I drove together from the Netherlands to Switzerland on a tight schedule only to discover the problem of a missing passport at the last possible moment!

At that time, the passport was an absolute requirement. Hearts sinking, hopes dashed, already in the lane leading to the gate house, we approached the border patrol, knowing full well that we were about to be turned back. Oh the stupidity of a moment's distraction! It seemed the passport lay forgotten on a table somewhere in France. From out of nowhere, a crack in time occurred. Simply, gently, naturally, a problem manifested right before our eyes, diverting police attention from our little red harp-laden car to that of another with a bleating cargo! The rickety truck filled with sheep and goats directly in front of us caused an unexpected commotion on an otherwise mild morning. Suddenly people were swarming and the place was awash in action. The police bounded to the driver's window waving and yelling: *move it or lose it, get out of the way!* They forgot to ask for the passports!

Gidi didn't quite believe that what had just happened was real, and sat staring blankly for the briefest moments, only to have them yell at us more loudly. Those kinds of direct openings that blossom in the midst of chaos occurred often in this project. From the quality of this passage, we surmised that this might be an indication of things to come. A certain quality of opening in the face of human failing—this characteristic has given us a lot of material for reflection as well as a strengthening of faith.

During that first visit, in the 1980s, Gidi served as translator much of the time because I didn't understand the Swiss dialect. In the privacy of Joa's home, we saw the original mystical paintings of the angels, of Mary, music, and more. Joa taught the two of us, a Jew and a Christian, new ways to pray. In a matter of hours, we learned of the burning necessity to publish her work in English. The only promise I ever made to Joa occurred in that hour. There wasn't much to do but reply to the moment as a destiny assignment. I told her I would do whatever it took to bring the legacy into print. (One simply does that when shaken to the core, not knowing what the big "yes" will entail.) Later, before we prepared to leave, Joa told us simply and naturally that she had seen the two of us in vision coming from the mountains about nine months earlier, but hadn't known who we were or why we would come, only that she could see our figures approaching. That wasn't the first or the last time one of us on the championing or publishing team rediscovered the value of staring down at our feet in moments of speechlessness. This second characteristic of being humbled beyond words is yet another current that pervades the whole endeavor and the lives of those who worked to bring the dream into reality.

For a good while during the next couple of years, I presented a manuscript of this first volume to publishers on both American coasts to no immediate avail. We had to persevere. My research assistant Sandy LaForge at Regis University and later at the Chalice of Repose Project helped me unhesitatingly to place copies of Joa's manuscript into the hands of key American editors and agents. She was the Xerox queen, spending hours lovingly copying, collating, and binding. In those days, *So That You May Be One* was formatted in such a way that the spaciousness and the quietude that pervades the vision experience was visually and generously represented on the page. It thus consisted of two oversize tomes, each spiral-bound, with hundreds of pages. Copies were carried in extra luggage to every city and placed directly in the hands of key readers. Each and every single graduate student that I taught and even some faculty members were involved and inspired. Everyone from the janitor to the dean contributed to a "Joa fund" with large checks and powerful "widow's mite" checks in order to help us continue to bring her work to the attention of American publishers. This third characteristic, a combination that Joa's work elicited from people—open generosity, dedicated involvement, trust of the new and gratitude to be of service—these elements made me realize each semester how much the American spirit actually contributed to the possibility of bringing her work to the fore.

The publishers' responses will come as no surprise to readers. They received telephone calls and approaches with great initial enthusiasm. But then, for some houses, Joa was too orthodox; for others, not enough. For some, too Protestant; for others, too Catholic, too subjective, too rigorous. For others, she was too biblical; for others, too radical, too unsettling. "Get rid of Mary and keep Jesus." "Can't you keep Jesus and get rid of the Bible?" "Her message is too demanding!" "Aren't there some easier visions?" There was a trade publishing world that was interested in books on meditation, but not necessarily prayer. Another constituency wanted books on spirituality but tended to overlook *Christian* mysticism in favor of psychological and self-help works. Third, great publishing houses sought scholarly works on the mystics, but usually those from earlier times, focused on individuals more easily identified securely in one tradition, not three! Ultimately, I believe it is to Joa's credit that she fit into no niche or slot. Nevertheless, she believed through the message of the angel that the American English-speaking world could receive the content of the visions at this time.

I don't know that this grass roots harbinger effort would have been possible for me to sustain in the United States without the unconditional assistance and understanding of Robert Sardello. His support and insight seemed to come out of the blue in 1990, but of course was providential. He immediately recognized the authenticity of her work, and gave me the moral support to be faithful to a wide-eyed promise made even while stumbling through a forest of brambles. After considering a number of places and also putting himself on the line in many other ways, it was Robert who first identified Lindisfarne Press and Christopher Bamford as a perfect fit. Christopher and I were familiar with each other professionally, but had not worked together publishing. With Chris, it was immediately clear and simple. Fluent in several languages and himself a person of prayer, he lavished devotion and insight into the work.

The color plates of the icons in the first volume were made possible through the generosity of a philanthropist who is a personal friend of mine and also a painter, a woman of spirit and prayer. It is her wish to remain anonymous. Several other American benefactors contributed anonymous funds to underwrite the costs of the production. This open-hearted giving and capacity to work quietly behind the scenes is a fourth pervasive characteristic. So many people beyond the mystic and the translator contributed to making this work available and beautiful, and we are in error for having missed the opportunity to acknowledge and remember them formally until now! Without each person's generosity and dedication, these books might not have seen the light of day in the English speaking world in Joa's life time. We wanted Joa to know while still alive in this world that God's presence, through the visions and messages, would be available to new readers, searching and hungry, at a time in history when humans need spiritual dew!

Meanwhile, there are still other dedicated people not mentioned by name in this preface, equally important, equally part of the Joa legacy, and by extension, the Johannine stream—praying, sacrificing, conforming themselves to God's will, consciously decreasing, making room for the light of another to increase. One woman so deeply and directly loved Joa's work that she did her thesis on the *visionlieder;* another cheered from the periphery by being supportive to the editors; both women died recently, as young women, in the prime of life.

All of the people involved in the first volume have been deeply changed by the commitment to make this legacy available. We each considered ourselves grateful to have been involved at any step along the way. Ultimately, on the American side, the first volume took a total of seven years of work after Joa and John Hill handed me the manuscript. During that time, numerous additional trips were made to Switzerland, Miriam Mason assisted greatly with translations then, and some of us helped things along with a documentary for Swiss television that asked questions about Joa, conducted interviews, and more. More recently, in August of 1998, the Americans Robert Sardello and Cheryl Sanders, deans of the School of Spiritual Psychology in Greenboro, North Carolina, positioned Joa to receive (by proxy) a meaningful Sophia Award at an international conference-retreat held at an Irish

Benedictine monastery. With the celebration of the Mass as the center piece of each day, this award recognized Joa's charism and wisdom. People from many lands flew in and gifted the woman mystic who to this day remains anonymous, who hobbles to a small village church and returns to her room to write and paint what she sees and hears.

Conversations with the Risen Ones

Following that first volume, we now have *Alive in God's World.* It is completely different from its predecessor, in content and methodology, yet a natural outgrowth of the first book. The Joa Bolendas of this volume still cherishes the living book of the Bible, and still receives Christ, Mary, the saints and angels. Her converse is in heaven. But something new is presented in the companion volume. It is intensely human and far more auditory. It takes a long time to realize that *Alive in God's World* is less about visual visions and more about spirit conversation, interior dialogue, and linking the communities of the living and the dead (the Risen Ones) into one living circle spanning time and space. The second volume does not contain the finite contents of visions such as might be found in the works of Hildegard, Mechthild, Teresa of Avila, or others. Briefly, Hildegard will see a vast world presented in a living image—concentric circles of angels, a woman stretching across the heavens whose gown is perfect on one side and torn on the other. She then writes in her diaries what this living image symbolizes, as given to her to know via prayer or the direct instruction of the spiritual world. The vision may or may not include words or music. The content of *Alive in God's World* is less visual and less allegorical, more auditory and more interpretive than *So That You May Be One.* (There are far fewer symbols, for example.) It is a document that shares deep, prolonged conversations between the Risen Ones and Joa. It isn't right to call these Risen Ones "saints," although the early church fathers addressed all the faithful as saints, whether or not on earth. *Alive in God's World* is the fruit of an intensely creative collaboration between a small number of people who *pray* to God and ask questions over

time, who *seek answers* or guidance to the problems of the day—
an endeavor that stands in marked contrast to the simultaneously
personal and private legacy of the prayer that pervades the mystic's
life, losses, and capacity to love.

The death of Joa's son Peter and the deaths of several other
people close to her eventually led her *personally* into the ultimate
Christian mysteries of death and resurrection. Joa never actually
despaired (she told me this) but, immersed in lamentation, she
faced dark waters and found a way to cross them. From grief, she
was broken open in new ways, but her mourning turned to joy.
Many years ago she developed the capacity to see, to hear, and to
receive those who have undergone what the world here calls death.

This second volume, true to the message of Christ's resurrection, reminds us that there is life beyond biological death, and that
death here is birth into a new life in a new form and dimension,
made possible because the Son of God vanquished death! Joa *sees*
how life-filled these beings are in their new state, and calls them
"Risen Ones." She hears them, hears their thoughts and musings,
clear ones and befuddled ones, and speaks to and with the souls of
the dead, spiritually. While volume one does include conversations
with the Risen Ones, the content of *Alive in God's World* docu-
ments extended dialogues with a variety of beings and describes
the *experiences* of the Risen Ones more fully and personally. However, in saying that, these dialogues never occur in the sense of a
séance—desire for contact with the dead has never forced open
the conversations, like hot house flowers in a greenhouse. The
source of these conversations and capacities is rooted in prayer:
daily prayer, sustained for decades, rooted in her Swiss Reformed
Protestant Bible readings, open and alive, grace-filled.

These Risen Ones communicate themselves to Joa in their own
ways, in the condition of their own souls, unique and particular
to the lives they led on earth—a painter, a musician, a scholar,
a rogue. These beings are relaying truthfully and authentically
their impressions and struggles, purgations and crownings, joys
and radiances, opinions and questions, from places less whole and
more whole, in other words, *as they truly are*. This might be one
of the most important indications that these conversations are

genuine: the Risen Ones with whom Joa has conversed are not perfect by any stretch of the imagination, but they are growing and seeking God in more and more real ways.

Additionally, there are what one might call "personality moments" that remain when a newly Risen One speaks shortly after life on earth. The longer they exist "in God's world," the less and less that fleeting, personality-laden, curious, unessential self speaks, and the more an eternal essential voice emerges, irradiated with light. The Risen Ones express themselves in ways not unlike ours, with varying degrees of truth, each according to their ability to see and to hear and comprehend a larger picture! They speak in ways limited and expansive, troubled and clear, somber and warm, humble and dignified, searching and finding, innocent and brave, fully human while fully spiritual. They describe in different ways how they are each growing into Christ, making room for His indwelling in their newly spiritualized hearts and bodies. It is as though they are showing us a kind of heavenly progressive incarnation, although that sounds like a contradiction in terms. Their growing into their newness occurs slowly and in stages, not rigidly delineated, but a true progression nonetheless. One hesitates to verbalize their heavenly embodiment. They come in a body of light, and to say more than that is perhaps folly.

Binding, Loosening, and Cherishing

This second volume differs from the first because the pages no longer relate pure visions in the finite traditional sense. The visions of Hildegard, for example, come to us in finite texts. They are "fixed." The scribe Volmar notated what she experienced. The nuns at Helfta helped gather the visions of Mechthild, who spoke them to sister scribes only under a vow of obedience, at the abbess's request. The texts of these visionaries are dynamic and living today, but we cannot telephone Hildegard or Mechthild or walk with them to chapel, asking for elaborations on their visions of the three harps, the ladder of gold, or the ten-stringed psaltery. The text is "fixed." The most we can do today is study primary texts, look at scribal hands, do comparative readings of textual variations. Then scholars link these findings to the various currents of biography, Scripture, and culture which shed light on the mystic's interior experience.

To contrast that, however, with Joa Bolendas is to describe not only a kind of extended grace period, but an extended creative period. The world the mystic sees, hears and receives is the fruit of intense and sustained collaboration between Joa and heaven, Joa and friends or even strangers suffering or struggling with real problems, sorrows and concerns in modern life: betrayal, shame, divorce, anger, hardness of heart, guilt, health, and more. People bring the raw materials of life and death to her and she in turn brings them to God. Then too, there is the border of epistemology and interpretation. What comes through human filter and what is pure revelation? This is where perseverance, acuity, and sensitivity are required.

At another level, Joa and John Hill have prayed together every week for years. This means that they will sit quietly in the rear of the church, Joa will receive a vision, a message, write a few words on small slips of paper, and John will pray with her. Whenever the timing is right, he is able to ask her questions and these questions in turn fructify and fortify her own further prayers. She returns to God, that day or another day perhaps a week later. This sensitive process continues. Sometimes John will pick up a thread a year later, and bring it, prayerfully, seeking wisdom and ultimately, God's will. Joa will sometimes begin, enter into an experience, and discover additional dimensions of the message only much later, in God's time.

Gidi Croes and I have also, at various times over the years, been able to sit with Joa and pray while the little scraps of paper pass from her hand to ours, as have Christopher Bamford and Robert Sardello. Once in 1997, she told me to leave the pew, stand up, open the palms of both hands, raise them, and rest them as well as my head on what appeared to daylight eyes as an unremarkable pillar at the rear of the church. That's how my soul originally heard it—the small way, the literal way. It took a while to understand her request in the deeper sense. In order to take the next step, she was asking me to *lean on a pillar of the church*. There was far more present than chiseled stone, and the authority of this command ushered me into a new life. How long it takes us to understand the significance of the most humble gestures, the smallest sentence, or an assignment that can seem to a fogged spirit a negligible task! I found my literal way, groping for stone, not understanding that she was asking me to enter into a living relationship with someone in the history of Christianity. More deeply than ever before, *I am leaning on a pillar of the Church.*

Then there is yet a third level of collaborative work. Even as editors, we have been allowed to ask questions about passages that were new, confusing, ambiguous, or even "limited" to the "simplicity" (!) of Joa's own life. At times, Joa would receive more in prayer, thus shedding light *on* a particular theme, or *through* the layers of *our* personal limitations. One year during Holy Week, Chris, John, and I followed the sun and met from early morning to late each evening, reciting the texts out loud, asking each other questions of linguistic, theological and cultural significance, reworking every word or phrase that called for clarification, going over the German and the Swiss German two and three times, wrestling with possible and alternate English renderings that would best convey the spirit of the original vision experience. It is safe to say that like all things of this nature, the shake up and awesome responsibility continues. What sections were too personal? What sections and experiences serve the greatest good when shared with a world hungry for meaning and authenticity? We truly labored over these questions, for they required far more than mere personal opinion. It is good to struggle and to grow, to be asked to *be* with the deep unknown and unknowable, the truly new, even while we attempt to describe Joa's intimacy and communion with Christ, John the Evangelist, Mary, and the saints.

The Significance of the Risen Ones Here and Now

What is the significance of Joa's reception of the Risen Ones? Many years ago, we know, for example, from the *Liber Specialis Gratiae* of Mechthild that she also was able to see how the Risen

Ones are *alive* in new and different ways, how they depend on our prayers and more, and how they are available to us spiritually. One can cite many other such historical examples of the saints in converse with those no longer physically embodied. In the classics of western Christian spirituality, sometimes a troubled soul going through purgation will appear to a saint; sometimes a human soul who is gleaming will appear and tell a saintly mystic about the glory of God. This is true in Benedictine, Cistercian, Carmelite, Franciscan and Dominican texts. But our age is a literal one, a statistical one, and we tend to concretize our experiences. In this way, we have perhaps forgotten about the presence of the "dead"— the presence of spiritual beings—in the normal daily activities of our lives, and maybe fall incomparably short in merely missing our loved ones and grieving over the seeming loss of those who have "died." Like the Gospels and like the classics of mysticism just cited, Joa's converse in heaven shows death as a birth into another world. What is radical about her communion with these souls is the arc of what we can only call "time" that is spanned. As in the life we know here on this side, each person grows in different ways and at different paces. This is verified also in heaven, although the element of time is replaced by space.

My own relationship to the care of the dying (and to the experience that accumulates from having attended many deathbed vigils) is spiritually and firmly rooted in the original Cluniac Benedictine practice of monastic medicine. At Cluny, something new happened: the impulse to link the community of the living with what one now (from the limitation of a modernist perspective) calls the community of the dead (meaning the Risen Ones). When this orientation is available, it of necessity sensitizes us to simultaneous realities regarding life and death and the language used in order to be faithful to both of those realities, not just one. For me, this orientation makes the readings of Joa's conversations with the Risen Ones who have died to this form a particularly fertile and burningly chaste endeavor. I have begun to learn a great deal about the reason and the poignancy of this aspect of Joa's charism with the Risen Ones, directly and obliquely, quietly and painfully, joyously and wondrously, with struggle and acceptance.

This full spectrum from concern to certitude and all the possible variations in between that I experienced personally, professionally, intellectually, and spiritually has required time and yet served a great good.

The three editors bring different and overlapping disciplines and personal orientations to the fore especially with these conversations with the Risen Ones. They bring different degrees of theological, psychological, spiritual, clinical, and personal experience to the table. Because of music-thanatology and the Chalice of Repose Project, I stand in a particular professional and vocational position in this domain. There is the position of extensive *experience* with the unbinding process of the dying and the converse with spiritual presences that sometimes occur as opposed to clinical theory or abstraction, romantic idealism or hardened cynicism; the position of *participation* with the one who is dying, rather than a procedural or purely clinical distancing; the position of having received countless unsolicited *testimonial notes* and letters from people who have survived the loss of their loved ones. They write to share deeply religious and spiritual experiences that happened at the deathbed and later, these include heavenly converse, and also to ask burning questions about such experiences and presences, and to thank us for our work. Last, and not the least valuable, there is the position of having been able to reflect on a huge body of experience provided by twenty-eight years of work in a mysterious yet practical field of medicine.

When these elements are coupled with an inexhaustible historical spiritual Tradition, you find at the very least the possibility of discerning, acknowledging and integrating the subtle signs and presences that naturally follow deathbed vigils and transitions. In John Hill's Jungian practice, he has counseled many people who have experienced soul death. In our music-thanatology clinical practice in Missoula, we work with biological death. As editors, the three of us have each known the losses of those close to us— maybe even closer to us than we have been to ourselves. This nuances things, ups the heat in the crucible, and not only fortified us to ask questions about difficult passages but maybe even *allowed* such questions to come to the fore with an authenticity devoid of curiosity. My own sense of things is that the editorial process for us has been nothing less than a further education and awakening.

All these individual and shared dimensions provided the deep convictions necessary to bring this effort to completion. Joa's message about life, change, and the *great life* has significance for our time and all time. I can't help thinking that this gleaming and creative picture stands in marked fecundity on its own but especially in contrast to the specter of Dr. Kevorkian and physician-assisted suicide. Just this week, while writing this preface, I received a daily European newspaper that described how the Dutch Parliament voted to legalize euthanasia. Although euthanasia is a choice that is more widely practiced than is openly admitted, the Netherlands is the first country in the world to legalize the possibility. The bill passed in Holland by a landslide vote of 104 to 40, and is expected to win approval in the Senate shortly. This vote approves euthanasia for children as well as adults, and is expected to go into effect in the early part of 2001, just as this book comes off the press.

One can't help but ache over the dilemmas that are afoot. In the United States, physician-assisted suicide remains extremely controversial. If the very real human experiences of despair, loneliness, fear of unmitigated pain and suffering, and ultimate loss of meaning could be helped, comforted, or transformed by a larger picture, a message of hope, then the timing of the release of *Alive in God's World* will bear quiet, golden fruit in the invisible orchards of human choice.

Joa Bolendas Serves the Johannine Church

Finally, it is a matter of conscience to link the life, work, and charism of Joa Bolendas to that of the Johannine Church, to the entire corpus of Johannine texts, and to both Johns—John the Beloved and John the Baptist. The reasons for this are several and simple, personal and professional, theological and mystical, measured and transparent. This Johannine mystical orientation and commitment isn't in opposition to the Petrine Church or the

Pauline Church—it is simply and truly *Johannine*. As many have noted, the Bible is not a single book, but rather an entire library, a whole world bound into one volume, yet the Book of Revelation is the last book within the Book, a sort of gleaming crown. Scholars aren't always united in their deductions when they trace the provenance of this crown, but that doesn't stop the stream from movement, flow, and life. Although it may be the least understood part of the New Testament, Revelation is the *only* prophetic book in the Christian corpus, and even if this takes some readers by surprise, Joa has long understood herself as a prophet.

You may remember from *So That You May Be One* that Joa is a person who saw world catastrophes (wars, earthquakes, Chernobyl) long before they occurred. Her response was not fear but compassion, courage, and more intensified prayer conversation with heaven. She asked everyone in her circle to stop what they were doing; this meant temporarily disrupting employment situations as well as personal plans. She asked them to storm heaven in prayer. As if from another time period, she asked members of her biological and extended family, young and old, to travel to different parts of the world (desert, mountain, shore and plain) to pray, bringing down grace like lightning rods and so perhaps curtailing or amending the consequences of our darkened human choices.

Joa's real prophetic charism links her to the Johannine prophetic tradition in the Book of Revelation, not because either of them preaches an end, but perhaps because they foresee a way to the New Jerusalem! *The Spirit and the Bride say, Come!* The New Jerusalem is a holy picture, where what has been separate becomes united and whole. The methodology of that transformative mysticism is taught directly and explicitly in Revelation. God's Word will be sweet on the tongue and bitter in the stomach. Digesting God's Word will cause an inner revolution; it causes a change in consciousness. The old encrusted sleeping parts of our religious lives that may in fact prevent a living spirituality are called into question and that is never comfortable. Even if or when we ultimately disagree with a detail, a content, or a perspective in Joa's world, the disagreeing, if done with grace, trust, and in love, has made us stronger and clearer. That contributes to the making of faith, and seems to me to be part and parcel of a Johannine teaching. The young and tender John was the only one who was strong enough of heart to stand vigil with Mary underneath the Cross. Later, he is one of the first to experience the Risen Christ in wide awake consciousness. Finally, the elderly John has one essential message at the end of life: love one another.

Joa's finest hours ring like a countermelody to, for, and around that which is intrinsically Johannine: a hidden world; a pseudonymous world; a hidden church; a listening world; a world that listens to the heart of Christ; a world that recognizes the significance of Jesus and that of His death and resurrection while they are happening; the primacy of God's Word in creation, healing, and salvation; an embodied world, irradiated with light; the capacity to be named and known as a Beloved; intimacy with the God of love; a primal light; Christ's increasing indwelling in our bodies, souls, and spirits; intimacy with Mary; the capacity to say "yes" to the impossible; a eucharistic life of thanksgiving and reverence; direct contact; a life utterly stripped of power.

I love and cherish the visible Church, as well as her many servants, lay and religious, over the arc of time. Yet I also see with reverence and solemnity that the Book of Revelation portrays the New Jerusalem to be so constituted with the active, breathing, shining presence of God that *there is no temple in the heavenly city!* There's not even a need for one! *There is no visible church.* The Risen Christ radiates and permeates everything and everyone! The visible form of a church or a temple has disappeared and the City of God and her people have become one indivisible, comprehensive whole. From this, I understand that true change comes gradually from within, involving the deepest possible conversion and translucency, and resulting in a more blessed, harmonious, exterior culture. I will continue to find a way to *sing prayer from the future,* that interior change might begin to shine and the shining is made audible. Mysteriously, Joa's prayer life is ineffably strong and vital, not because of visions and auditions, but because of such unsullied, simultaneous, and chaste connections to both heaven and earth. She calls us to question our fragmented selves and any religious habit that has become formulaic, hard of heart, fearful or proud. In doing so, she shakes up several worlds. Then she tilts her little head of gleaming pure white hair, and returns to her desk to pray, as if it's simply all in a day's work.

Thus shaken, I stand corrected, reorganized, and thankful.

Missoula, Montana
Feast of the Immaculate Conception, 2000

Translator's Introduction
by John Hill

The visionary testimony of Joa Bolendas awakens us to the reality
of spiritual life on earth and in heaven. To be alive in God's world
is to live in a prayerful and powerful unity not just with God, but
also with those risen from the dead, and with all the peoples of the
earth. To live this unity is truly human. The visions in this book
bring awareness of the deep bonds uniting the living with each
other, with the dead, and with God. In fragmentary discourses,
the Risen Ones tell us of their new life in God's world. They tell
us to make God's kingdom alive on earth and so release a process of great spiritual energy to guide humanity and restore the
earth to its spiritual axis. Immanuel Kant once dismissed Emanuel
Swedenborg's visions on the afterlife as the work of a fanatic. An
examination of Swedenborg's life, however, reveals the character
of a man who was humble, discreet, and unassuming. No doubt
Kant, though believing in the immortality of the soul, was influenced by the general prejudice toward anyone who claimed to have
had experience of life after death. It is hoped that through meditation on the material in this book, the reader's soul can overcome
old fears and prejudices and warm to a new call to the life of the
spirit that extends beyond our short life on earth.

"Awaken, open your eyes, behold, you are truly alive." Such
words might express the mystery of this book. The life of an
individual is but a short day in the ongoing process of creation.
We can live according to the measurements of that one day, but
the messages received by Joa Bolendas lift us beyond and place
us in an unfolding universe to welcome a new morning. Through
the tragic death of her firstborn son, Joa Bolendas was called to
participate in his risen life. The unpublished visions that tell of this
event bear witness to a mother's heart opening up to the radiance
of the human spirit. The loving and searching openness of Joa's

dialogue with her son, a quality that permeates all the visions in this book, is a testimony to the full potential of human life on earth and in heaven.

As we approach the subject of this book—human life, death and immortality—it is difficult to define what kind of reality we are about to investigate. Does our search for a deeper understanding of death and an afterlife begin with an awareness of the finitude of life; with visible and tangible realities of sickness, death, corpses, memories and loss of our loved ones? We must ask ourselves if the dead have survived the grave and if they can be our invisible partners in our search for meaning. Can we create a dialogue with them? Can our images, projections, fantasies, longings, hope, and despair be answered, encouraged, criticized, denied, as dialogue in any partnership requires?

Perhaps we will not be able to answer all these questions, but the visionary narratives in this book may be understood as an appeal to be open to experiences with the dead and to evaluate them in terms of self-reflection, self-awareness, and the search for a life of meaning. Care is needed not to idealize, simplify, and thus anthropomorphize the continuity between the living and the dead. There is always an element of uncertainty in moving across the bridge that links the living with the dead. In the ancient religions of Persia, this bridge is imaged as a sharp sword, which cuts down all those who are unworthy to pass into the next life. The idea of continuity is in itself an abstraction and, if understood in a linear way, can flatten out the polarity, disruption, uncertainty, pain, and horror that accompanies the approach of death and the end of our life on earth. But if we live with this uncertainty—live fully in presence of suffering, degeneration of our bodies, and the pain of loss of loved ones—then continuity is no longer a flat ideology of sameness. Rather it is a process arising out of individual experiences of a life that is continually broken up, out of joint, and reassembled. This is a process of strengthening the spirit, a living with death and the dead, and a gathering of all those signs and messages that seem to communicate to us something about a life that is powerful enough to survive its disappearance from the human body.

A teacher of Buddhism once tried to emphasize a shift in human values by outlining two distinct ways to understand human nature. We understand ourselves either to be essentially human beings who undergo a spiritual experience or to be essentially spiritual beings who are undergoing a human experience. Unfortunately, the trend in contemporary civilization makes the process of understanding, nourishing, and strengthening the spirit very difficult, if not impossible. The continual influx of information about all the comforts and distractions that can alleviate pain, emptiness, and unhappiness divert us from the truth of our spiritual reality. The ever-increasing isolation from nature, the cementing over of environment, the building of monumental structures for the control and consumption of material wealth, the obsession with productivity—the list goes on—all these force us to live a lifestyle in which there is no time to stop, reflect, and ask ourselves what the point to it all is. Do we realize what part we have to play in a system in which we are one tiny unit with a short life in a perishable body? Things themselves are made to last far beyond an individual lifetime. But what about us human beings, who are the most perishable of all? What about *our* enduring? In our culture today, death has become taboo. We seem to be no longer able to erect visible signs to remind us of our own passing away, our dead ones, our ancestors. It is becoming increasingly difficult to find roots and be at home in this world because the world, as we know it today, no longer reflects our true selves, no longer reminds us that we are human beings with an identity that may outlast physical death. The artificial worlds we are creating no longer reflect the possibility of a continuity of life, both visible and invisible.

This was not always the case. It is well known that most peoples of early civilizations attempted to accompany their dead ones, using myth, artifact, or ritual, until they found rest in the next world. Anyone who has studied the peoples of earlier civilizations cannot but be impressed by their overwhelming concern about survival after death. These ancient peoples spared no means in erecting visible signs of a continued presence of the dead among the living. The vast burial mounds of Neolithic culture, the great pyramids of Egypt, the wooden stretchers of native Americans are visible and tangible embodiments of a continuous universe. All served to remind the living that the lands of the dead were near at hand. Thus the funeral rites of many cultures evolved around the notion of a journey undertaken by the soul of the dead person. The dead had to go on this journey to be united with their ancestors. Mourning rites provided a framework not only to allow the living to mourn the loss of the loved one but also to ensure the continued support of the living for the dead as they undertook their long journey to join the spirits of their ancestors. These rites entailed a suspension of all normal social life, a living with the corpse in wakes and ritualistic wailings, fasting, and meals. The transition periods of mourning might have lasted several months, sometimes years, gradually coming to a close with the final burial of the corpse and a return to social life, until the next death occurred. The people of those cultures lived a different life from the people of today. They were deeply aware of the reality of spirit, having spent much of their short lives in creating a symbolic space to accompany their dead.

Many of these customs and beliefs have continued to survive in all the great religions of the world. Christians throughout the ages have lived a life of denial and undergone great hardships and sacrifices in order to prepare themselves for eternal life. The issues of life beyond death and a community of the living and the dead (the "Communion of Saints") have always been of fundamental significance to the Christian experience. A great variety of images of the afterlife blossomed within this context. In the Middle Ages, for instance, heaven was imaged largely as a city resembling a Gothic cathedral and defined theologically in terms of a contemplative vision of the Godhead. In the Renaissance, artists and mystics imagined it to be a place of sensuous delight and enjoyment: a beautiful garden with flowers, trees, animals, fountains, in which the blessed danced, played, swam, bathed, and discussed with one another. Still later, through the influence of Swedenborg, it became a place where the blessed would be given tasks and continue to do good works as part of their spiritual progress. Heaven was envisioned as a state of love, not one in which a beatific vision alone sufficed, but one in which family and social relations blossomed, and through which God became known and glorified.

Among theologians in our times, however, a powerful reaction has developed against all-too-human conceptions of heaven and hell. The sometimes crude, simplistic, and concretistic images of a continuity of earthly life in heaven, which often reflected the cultural conditions of the times, have influenced theologians to reject literal conceptions of the afterlife. Tillich, Bultmann, and Rahner emphasize in different ways the radical distinction between the images, symbols, and myths of eternity and the actual temporal, psychophysical conditions of human life on earth. They emphasize that we have no direct knowledge of the next life and we are to avoid naïve literalism. Despite such risks, however, a nonsensuous, intellectual understanding of the afterlife hardly suffices to capture the imagination, hardly encourages modern man and woman to be moved and inspired beyond the concerns of everyday life, so as to perceive that liminal transitional space, in which there is a real linking of the living with the dead.

Today many of these older beliefs concerning death and renewal are to be rediscovered in the outpourings of patients and clients who find they can reveal the secrets of their soul in the protective and trusting atmosphere of psychotherapy. In the intimacy of a consulting room, imagery, thoughts, and experiences about survival after death may be discovered and explored in a transitional space, which has now ceased to exist as an outer social framework. I have been working as a Jungian analyst in Zurich for nearly thirty years. My patients, with their troubled lives, have formed much of my attitude to life. Inevitably the theme of death arises again and again. The dead appear in my patients' dreams, fantasies, and active imaginations. Very often they have helped patients at most critical periods of their lives.

I remember the case of a woman who had suffered severe abuse as a child. After years of analysis, she suddenly began to draw pictures of sarcophagi on which a stone figure in the shape of a young woman was placed. We had no difficulty in recognizing that the woman was the analysand herself. Through the violent abuse she had suffered, a whole section of her personality had been murdered, causing it to disappear into the underworld of her psyche, and was thus lost to consciousness. The only signs that something was buried in the depth of her unconscious were dreams of corpses and tortured animals, as well as tense moments of terrible irritability, fear, guilt, and shame. Through careful therapeutic work, the analysand could find trust in humanity once more. She began to draw pictures of herself as a young woman full of vitality—a clear sign that the stone figure on the sarcophagus was coming back to life again.

Each time a client embarks on such a journey, I stop and marvel at the incredible capacity of the psyche to bring back to life what was previously thought to be dead. I also stop and wonder if this intrapsychic process does not point to something deeper. When this happens, are we not witnessing the very foundations of the soul's immortality? Do not such experiences already imply the soul's capacity to survive physical death? There are other kinds of dreams and fantasies, which possess a visionary quality and which appear to point more clearly in this direction. They don't represent lost parts of the individual psyche, but have an existential quality informing us about survival after death, not only about ourselves, but also about our ancestors and loved ones, as the following examples show.

A patient of mine, for instance, was suffering from a relapse of cancer and was about to be operated upon. She was convinced her time had come. Just before the operation, her dead grandmother, for whom she had very positive associations, appeared in a dream, assuring her that all would be well. This appearance brought tremendous relief and my patient lost her fear of the illness and of death. She did in fact get better and there was no sign that the cancer would return. She was convinced that her beloved grandmother had returned from the realm of death to help her overcome despair.

Another patient had suffered from a major depression for nearly twenty years. He had been in analyses for many years. I was his second analyst. One day, he began to relax into a trance-like state of consciousness. Suddenly he began to wail. Previously, over many sessions, an old woman from the past, who claimed to be a distant ancestor, had explained to him that he held the key to redeem her sufferings and save "the child" who seemed to symbolize the survival of her family. Now slowly he realized that he was the "child" she had been talking about. She spoke in an old-fashioned dialect, different from the one this man used, telling him that all had been destroyed by a great famine in the land of his ancestors. She was caught in that terrible vision of death and destruction, and could not move on in the next world. My patient's suffering was her suffering. Only when he began to understand this and accept responsibility for an ancestral chain and for "the child" could the old woman let go and promise to no longer haunt him. After several weeks, the strange dialogue came to an end and the woman informed him that now that he had accepted her suffering, which was part of his own history and the history of his people, she was redeemed and could go to heaven. The event and the working through of another traumatic event in his personal life, finally and indeed unexpectedly, brought this man's major depression to an end. To the surprise of this man and myself, the old woman's promise did come true.

The following dream reveals in a startling and direct way, the soul's capacity to prepare us for physical death and for a further life beyond the grave:

> *I am tugging and pulling at a rubber inflatable dinghy of a gray rubbery color. I am trying to get it to fold up. I am making great efforts but nothing is happening. All of a sudden the dinghy becomes a small silver vessel, and a voice says: "This is the vessel of the spirit; treat it gently." I am holding the vessel in my two hands, and feel a great sense of peace.*

The dreamer was a fifty-year-old woman. She was dying from cancer in a nearby hospital. The dream was presented for group discussion. In the discussion, we could understand the dream as foretelling the woman's death. Indeed we were informed that her body, through the illness, had become all gray and rubberlike. The patient was hoping to die quickly so that she would not have to suffer. Jung once said that the unknown voice in a dream usually meant a voice from the Self—from the core of our personality. I

understood the silver vessel as being similar to those tiny ancient
Egyptian boats of precious metal. These vessels were to carry the
dead across the night waters of the Underworld, so that they are
reborn with the new sun. This mysterious dream was obviously
intended to inspire the dying woman toward a new attitude to
life beyond death. Her dying body was to be transformed into a
spiritual body. Through her dream, the woman was being prepared
to cross those dark waters that separate life from death in a gentle
and peaceful way, and thus assume a spiritual identity that could
survive the breakdown of her body.

Many dreams, visions, and near-death experiences encountered
today reveal modern man and woman's continual search for a
meaningful attitude toward death and survival. Let us not fall
a victim to old prejudices, but gather all these signs and messages
that tell us about the greater life beyond physical death. We need
to remember that most peoples of early civilizations attempted to
accompany their dead for a long time until they found rest in the
next world. Following them, for the last two thousand years countless theologians, poets, artists, and mystics have devoted much of
their energy to understand and make tangible visions of a life beyond death. Within this context we may appreciate the visionary
texts of Joa Bolendas in a fuller way, and thus open our hearts and
our minds to participate in the life of the Risen Ones.

The visions of Joa Bolendas, published here, have much to
say on the soul's progress in life after death. I have known Joa
Bolendas for more than thirty years. She is Swiss, Protestant, wife
of a pastor of the Reformed church, and mother of three children.
She is now over eighty years old and lives in retirement in an old
people's home.

Joa Bolendas' visions are not just the work of her own intellect
or imagination. She has described the process of receiving visions
as being in an infused state—infused with energy—that has a
quality of communication with some being other than herself.
Concomitantly, or sometimes shortly afterwards, she hears or sees
the words and images that accompany her infused state of being.
Joa has lived two lives. One was her commitment as a pastor's
wife, involved in the family and in the parish; the other was her

call as a visionary. Both have been founded on a love toward God and humanity.

Her visionary life started forty years ago and may be divided roughly into three parts. The early visions express her personal struggle to accept the gifts she had been offered. She never wanted visions. Often she was asked to do things that she would otherwise never have done, had she lived a normal life. The visions are essentially ecumenical, and Joa had to understand and integrate aspects of Christianity, such as the significance of icons, Mary, the saints, the rosary, and the mass, which were foreign to the traditional practices of her own Reformed church. Already in the early visions, a Johannine mysticism of Divine light, life and love, inherent in all being, is infused throughout the messages she received. The affirmation of a spiritual life, which is linked with God, Christ, and the Holy Spirit, and through which we are born to eternal life, is common to both the fourth Gospel and Joa's visions. Here is a promise of a fulfillment of human nature, expressed in a deep spiritual love of God and one's fellow human beings. According to the visions, the mystery is best experienced in the Eucharist. A Johannine understanding of Communion implies that, through the life of the risen Christ, the primal light of creation is passed on to human beings, strengthening them to participate in God's creation as people of light, now and in the afterlife. The second part of her visionary life focused on a Johannine transconfessional unity of the churches, of the peoples of the world, and of the forces of life in an individual. Much of this material has been published in the book: *So That You May Be One.*[1] The third and probably final part of Joa's work concerns the spiritual evolution of humanity, here on earth and in heaven. The visions, some of which are now published in this book, include testimonies of deceased people who have spoken to Joa in vision about their experiences of the afterlife.

The content of these conversations with the risen people of

---

1. Joa Bolendas, *So That You May Be One* (Hudson, N.Y.: Lindisfarne Books, 1997).

the afterlife elaborates on theological issues and is to be understood as an integral part of the overall message of Joa's visionary life. The visions are rooted in the Christian framework. Similar to the images of Orthodox Christianity, heaven, the afterlife, and the resurrection of the dead unfold within a theocentric framework. The Risen Ones in heaven open their eyes to the wonder and magnificence of creation, giving praise and thanks to the Creator. They continually encourage us to seek relationship with God, Christ, the Holy Spirit, Mary, the saints, and the angels. Despite the theocentric emphasis of heavenly life, heaven in Joa's visions is not just made up of solitary individuals contemplating the divine essence. In a manner similar to recent astronomical discoveries of the enormousness of the physical universe, God's heaven appears to be a vast and complex expanse, composed of many different realms. The people of these visions tell us that they are alive and continue to develop in heaven and, at the same time, maintain their presence on earth in an active, social way.

The most striking quality of Joa Bolendas' visionary accounts is the candid, matter-of-fact way the dialogues with the departed are held. Through these conversations, Joa Bolendas brings the inhabitants of heaven in close, almost tangible proximity. Similar to some of the earlier anthropocentric conceptions of heaven, the dead behave in very human ways. They express gratitude, are amazed at seeing things they had never seen before, need time to get used to their new surroundings, and are very concerned about their children, grandchildren, and the future of humanity. Much of what is witnessed corresponds to the reports of Raymond Moody.[2] Upon dying, the dead experience great peace and relief. They can see what is happening on earth, their body is transformed into a spiritual body of energy and light, they meet loved ones that have passed on before them, they are guided by beings of light, and they witness a review of their life on earth. Unlike the subjects of Moody's reports, however, the people of Joa's visions cross over the barriers separating the living from the dead, they do not return to their physical bodies, and they move

---

2. Raymond Moody, *Life After Life* (New York: Bantam Books, 1977).

into deeper dimensions of heavenly life. Love and the search for inner truth are of paramount importance to both Moody's reports and Joa's visions.

Despite the Christian emphasis of these visions, earlier ways of understanding life after death are not condemned but are appreciated as an integral part of human evolution. These ways are practiced still today in Buddhism, shamanism, and the ancestor worship of the Shinto religion. Nevertheless the resurrection of life, understood from a Johannine perspective, is to be distinguished from reincarnation and belief in the soul's eternal recurrence. The message here presented is eschatological in nature. It speaks about the final fulfillment of man and woman, even if the life of the resurrected human being is described as a state of continual activity and process.

The relationship between time and eternity remains a paradox. After death, risen man and woman can experience a whole lifetime, collective history, or periods of evolution in a condensed time-dimension, and begin to participate in a continuous unfolding of creation. The content of these visions may serve as an opportunity to translate contemporary visions of the universe, as a process of condensation and unending expansion, in terms of human consciousness. Henri Bergson has reminded us that states of the self are usually perceived through forms borrowed from the external world.[3] Consciousness cannot be understood by adding separate units of linear time, just as time cannot be reduced to a measurement of space. Care is needed not to confuse extension with duration, succession with simultaneity, and quantity with quality. The first are the properties of matter, the second of mind. According to Bergson, the quality of consciousness can be grasped in those serious moments of decision where there is an interpenetrating of psychic states, in which "their dynamic unity and wholly qualitative multiplicity are phases of our real concrete duration, a heterogeneous duration and a living one."[4] In the visions of Joa Bolendas, time references are not to be

3. Henri Bergson, *Time and Free Will* (New York: Harper & Row, 1960), p. 223.
4. Ibid., p. 239.

understood within a linear framework, but imply a duration of ever-deepening interiority, in which psychic states of an increasing multiplicity undergo an equivalent condensation. The visions indicate that human consciousness, once linked with God, undergoes a transformation, through which events in time become progressively subsumed under the auspices of a duration that embraces a mysterious totality, hardly to be grasped with normal consciousness.

According to the Gospels, Christ came not to destroy but to fulfill. The gift of eternal life is but a further development of those countless myths and rituals, created by man and woman to ensure survival after death. With the new creation outlined in the New Testament, humans no longer need embalming, belongings, or artifacts to ensure their passage into the next world. Yet similar to the older cultural patterns, the saints and angels of Joa's visions tell us that we are to accompany the dead with our prayers as they undertake their long journey through the realms of heaven. The dead need not worry to whom they were married or to whom they will be married, for those who attain resurrection take neither wife nor husband (Luke 20:34–36). However, Joa Bolendas has seen that a deep spiritual love, which has developed between man and woman while they lived on earth, does survive in the afterlife and becomes part of eternity. It is not the physical body, but a transformed spiritual body of energy that is alive in heaven. The new link with God through Christ is not to be understood as an abstract ideal, but as a living reality. Saint John's testament grasps, through a symbolic understanding, the living quality of the risen life when he tells us to eat and drink the bread and water of eternal life. Thus the Godhead will dwell within us. Only the spirit gives life (John 6:64) and this life force, which perhaps makes physical life possible in the first place, is not subject to the laws of corruption and death.

If we are to speak of heaven, then it is certainly not a heaven modeled on patriarchal society. It is not a place where men run the show and women serve. Neither is it a place filled with pious virgins. Nor does it mirror an all too human tendency to bathe in self-righteousness, splitting good and evil and projecting evil on all those who are opposed to us, as can be implied in some traditional images of heaven and hell. With the breakdown of the patriarchal power structures in the churches and in society and the gain of a new freedom for men and women, a corresponding change in our imagery of the next world is taking place. The visions here presented tell us that man and woman are made in the image and likeness of God and that God's heaven is exciting, open, alive and human.

Resurrected life is not to be understood as a quality of space. All too often Christian iconography has illustrated life after death as a place—heaven, hell, or purgatory. Heaven is but a further dimension of resurrected life, and resurrected life is but a further dimension of human life and is to be appreciated in terms of a continuity of individual consciousness. Neither should resurrection be understood from a purely temporal point of view. It is not just something to happen in the future, after death. Christ's death and resurrection changed the pattern of creation and cut right through the division between the living and the dead. Eternal life, given by God through Christ, unites the living and the dead. The people of Joa's visions exhort us over and over again to link our lives with God and Christ and thus, while still alive on earth, we are born into eternal life. We are to share that life with all human beings whether they are alive on earth or in heaven. Death may never lose its sting, but we learn the sting does not have to be final. The visions of Joa Bolendas help us catch a glimpse of the other side and thus further our understanding of death as a point of transition, in which life appears to be shattered, recovers in God's world and begins to blossom in a new way.

Joa Bolendas experienced the transition through death with great hardship and intensity. On the third of May 1965, her eldest son, Peter, had a car accident. Joa herself did not want the visions concerning that event to be included in the book, because of their intensely personal nature. She feared that they might detract from the overall intention of this work, which is to emphasize the variety of experiences open to individuals as they try to understand the loss of loved ones or as they prepare themselves to pass through the doors of death to risen life. There is no one model for this kind of transition. She saw many times that the separation of body and soul is an experience unique to every individual, requiring each time a different attitude, different support, and different prayers.

She did, however, experience the suffering and anguish of a mother who has lost her son. In a unique way she tried to come to terms with the will of heaven. Despite her great loss, Joa Bolendas was reassured over and over again that the love between her and Peter could not be broken by death. In truth this love took on new meaning. The experience of the death and resurrection of Peter transformed Joa's whole life, prepared the ground for a deeper committed conviction about her calling and her work, and helped her understand the full significance of the truly human and of the greater life beyond death.

This Translation

The original German text was privately printed in 1998. I have used that text as the basis for the present translation. "Risen from the Dead" was printed in 1982, and first published in English in 1997 in *So That You May Be One*. This introduction continues at the beginning of various sections of this book.

Joa Bolendas' style of writing is direct, spontaneous, and at times telegraphic. Its beauty lies in its simplicity. It is not the language of the Greek or Latin theologians. It is not a language of definitions. Joa Bolendas receives answers that explain not just what things are, but also what they do. According to Hans Küng, this kind of language is closer to the spoken language of biblical times.[5] Wherever possible, I have tried to retain this original style. Changes have been made only where the full meaning could not be contained in a direct rendering of the German text—and these changes only with the permission and help of the author. It should be noted that words in brackets were not directly spoken in the visions, but were implied. It is also important to remember that much space lies between these words. I have often sat in a church

---

5. Hans Küng, *On Being a Christian* (London: Fount Paperbacks, 1989), p. 46.

with Joa Bolendas for more than an hour, during which time she wrote down a mere five to ten lines of vision. Most of this time was spent in beholding a spiritual presence in prayer and silence. I would like to express my gratitude to the team of editors who, besides myself, included Christopher Bamford and Therese Schroeder-Sheker. Without their inspiration and support, this edition of Joa's work would not have been possible. My special thanks to Lela Fischli, Simon Mason, and Miriam Mason for their valuable help in the translation.

Part One

ALIVE ON EARTH: IN GOD'S IMAGE AND LIKENESS

"A new beginning!" With these words addressed to Joa Bolendas, Mary, the mother of Jesus, introduces a dimension of human existence long recognized to be an essential part of human identity, difficult to grasp, understand, or believe.

The overall purpose of this work is to serve as a testimony to the fullness of human nature on earth and in heaven. God's creation of humanity on earth, and God's intention for humanity in heaven is witnessed as a single existence. The larger part is devoted to the full blossoming of God's creation and therefore is concerned with experiences beyond our short life on earth. Nevertheless, Joa Bolendas insisted that some visions about the fullness of life on earth be included. She knows that her testimony in this section cannot be comprehensive, but she believes such context is necessary. Further visionary material—which also helps contextualize what is given here—has already been published in *So That You May Be One*. The visions in this volume focus on what it means to be human. The final fulfillment of men and women in heaven can be understood in terms of the gradual evolution of the human soul and spirit while still embodied on earth.

We must remember that Joa Bolendas is not writing about

her ideas. Her testimony comes from a gift of vision, given by God. She struggled against these messages for years; similarly each reader is to question and struggle with the visions to recognize what they mean in his or her own life. During the past forty years, Joa Bolendas' whole life has been nourished and transformed by these visions. Their content is not to be understood as a full explanation of human nature. In one vision, Mary, the mother of the Lord, told Joa that she had only seen a fragment of the whole of existence. The visions simply point to the immensity of creation, and of human nature on earth and in heaven. They bring to life the potential of what we can be. This potential is presented in the fragmentary narratives of people known to Joa, who have risen from the dead. There are probably as many different narratives as there are stars in the heavens.

The visions begin with the first thousand years of human existence on earth. Through the words of Mary, Joa witnesses primal humanity's awakening to the reality of its own transcendence, achieved through bodily movement and orientation toward the heavens. With the dawning of consciousness came recognition of the different levels of energy and of the human as truly human. In the images of the first human being, born from an animal yet remaining a creation of God, evolution and creation are presented as complementary principles. Kinship with the animals, full affirmation of sexuality, and the daily rhythmic balance of embodied devotion to life of the spirit, to work, and to community life are all aspects of the first blossoming of human existence on earth.

– 1 –

The First Thousand Years of Human Life

While I was praying, Mary appeared, looked at me in a questioning way, and said:

Open your eyes.
A new beginning!

I saw a man standing, quiet and relaxed, in an open space. He was holding both hands before his face, palms turned inward, loose and slightly cupped. They did not touch his face. After a period of stillness, the man lowered his hands to the level of his chest. He spread out his arms slowly until he was completely stretched out. Then he moved his arms back to the center of his body, cupping his hands over his belly. After another period of stillness, he opened his hands again and stretched out his arms at the level of his hips. Then he slowly brought them back to the front of the body where the torso ends. Another period of stillness. And again he opened his hands, this time stretching his arms far apart at the level of his knees and then, bending his back, bringing them together at his feet. Finally, he stood up and looked toward the sun.

Then Mary spoke:

The man was looking toward the sun.
A few looked toward the moon,
others to the stars.
Thus human beings attained a greater consciousness
of something beyond them.
(*There was not yet any concept of God.*)
This was the first awareness of the human as human.

First the head, then the chest and arms,
the torso, the hips (*movement*), sexuality,
the knees, which were important for moving and climbing,
and the feet, which had to be coordinated with each other.
This was consciousness of the harmony of different powers.

This slow-moving exercise, which they did morning and evening,
was the first conscious act of self-perception
on the part of human beings:
to recognize and affirm themselves as human.
It took place in the first thousand years of human life on earth
and was part of human development.
It distinguished human beings
from all other creatures on earth.
Traces of these movements and postures
may still be found today!

*After these visions, I asked Mary why she had shown me these visions.
She said:*

You—human beings today—
bear five million years
of informative patterns[1] within you.
The first human beings
were without this inheritance.
Therefore they had to begin with
observing themselves, beholding themselves.
This was the coming to consciousness
Of human beings—as humanity!

---

1. The German word *Informationen* has no one accurate English equivalent. *Informationen* appear to be coded patterns that inform the entirety of creation. "Informative patterns," "codes," "impulses" are approximate translations, suggesting much of the original meaning. (See p. 16.)

– 2 –
The Birth
of the First Human Being

Mary continued:

Let us observe human evolution together, step by step.
Do not hurry.
Observe all this exactly as you observed
how humans became conscious of themselves.

The human being was born—created
as a human, not an animal.

The cells—the first cells, the coming into being of human cells—
are a unique creation by God:
God's conscious creation of the human being.

The first human developed and came to term
after nine months of pregnancy
in a gentle animal resembling the human.

– 3 –

The Parting
of Humans and Animals

Mary spoke:

The "first" to the "third" human beings
lived with the animals.

Two years after this vision, someone asked if this referred to individuals, generations, or types of primates. I asked about this. Luke the Evangelist answered:

The first three humans whom you were told about
refers to the first three "generations."
It was a shorthand way of saying it.
These three "generations" were from the same clan.

Then Mary continued:

It was their way of running and climbing,
and their upright posture
that outwardly distinguished
the first human beings from the animals.

The human species separated from the animal world.
Communities, humans, came together, formed independent clans,
and gave birth to humans only!

This happened in the first three "generations."
Then the human was above the animal.
The animal was beneath the human.
Human beings lived in nature
surrounded by animals.
An aura could be seen in and around human beings.
Thereby humans had a capacity
to absorb informative patterns, impulses.
They would often grasp their heads with their hands.
This indicated a moment of perception.
They would also move their feet—
especially the ball of the foot and the toes—with their hands:
this was also a moment of understanding.

And after another "generation,"
the animals began to separate from humans.
The animals moved on, retreated into the forests.

It was not humans who parted from animals,
but animals from humans!

Later, wondering about the account in Genesis 1:28, I asked about the power struggle between human beings and animals. An angel answered:

God created the earth,
the waters, the plants, and the animals.
Finally God created human beings!
Humans had to "overcome" the animals
in a struggle not with force
but with knowledge and intelligence.
Power could have intoxicated many animals so strongly
that they would have annihilated the human being.
But God gave humans love
as well as power on earth.
Pray that this power does not become sinful!

A scientist read my visions and asked if Darwin was right about the evolution of the species. A saint answered:

Yes—but when the evolution of species goes wrong,
and does not follow God's intention for creation,
then God brings change.
Think about the giant dinosaurs.

Is competition a basic law of creation? The saint answered:

No! Listen!
God's power in the universe is stronger
than "competition" on earth!
Creation is in God's hands!
Believe and pray!

– 4 –
Fire, Water, Air

Mary continued:

Fire—through lightning—
water—roaring water—
aroused terror, shock, and fear in human beings.
Storms, which shook the earth, confused them.

Primal forces, more powerful than humans,
transformed them over a period of "four hundred years."

– 5 –
Tears and Laughter

Mary spoke:

Men, women, and children
began to cry—to laugh!
They began to perceive and recognize
pain, suffering, joy, and happiness.

This was an important stage of development!

*When I suddenly saw how primal human beings laughed and cried,
I was deeply impressed about what had been achieved in evolution! I
think anybody would have felt the same way. Tears came to my eyes.*

– 6 –

Sexual Life
in the First Thousand Years

I was then shown how man and woman searched for one another and encountered each other. First of all, they did so with their eyes. When they were closer, the man caressed the surface of the woman's fingers and hands. After this contact, they touched each other with their foreheads. They caressed their cheekbones. Amorous with one another, they caressed the other's shoulders. Afterward, they caressed the front of the pelvis. Only then did their sexual parts touch. The sexual act could be gentle or fiery. After some time—a half an hour to an hour—they massaged their own knees with strong circular movements. It was only then that the sexual act was completed.

– 7 –

The Daily Rhythm of Life
in the First Thousand Years

I was shown how the first human beings consciously opened themselves up to the light with body and soul. From early morning until midday, they would squat down or move at intervals; their whole being was turned toward the light. I saw them with open arms—quiet, relaxed, and full of joy. At these moments they absorbed light and air. They lived in unity with life. They were filled with light until the middle of the day; it looked as if they had a fine vessel full of light in front of them. In the afternoon they did their heavy work, for example work with trees and water. Evening was a time of meeting with their family, their children, and loved ones. I saw the children stroking the heads of animals. Even a doll was shown to me, made from a simple wooden branch. These small dolls had open arms, also made from branches. Playing with the dolls, the children learned to relate. So I experienced their daily rhythm: morning—devotion to soul, spirit, and body; afternoon—heavy work; evening—encounters, community life, the expression of love for one another.

An angel spoke:

And they were healthy and happy.

– 8 –

Man and Woman

To be alive on earth is to live the unity of male and female. Neither men nor women alone define human nature. The visions imply that a fuller reality of human life becomes conscious in the conjoining of male and female in a deep union of love. This metaphysical unity may be realized in many different ways: in marriage, in friendship, in work, or as the experience of the union of male and female in a single soul. This kind of love is so powerful, so grounded in the very core of our being that it extends beyond life on earth and becomes part of eternity. In the creation of the human being, God has put male and female together. The injunction of the Evangelist—what God has joined let no man put asunder—is understood in a new way. We are not to destroy the human being made in the image and likeness of God. No one may break that whole apart.

26.7.1988
Once in vision, I saw that five million years had passed since God created the human being. This is an immense period of human evolution, yet throughout this period, a man has remained a man and a woman a woman. The problems in relationship between man and woman have not lessened but have only become greater. One day, after I had been

discussing marriage and divorce with several people, a saint appeared
in vision and spoke:

You see it wrong.
Man and woman form a unity.
This unity must not be destroyed through sin,
through evil intentions.

If unity has not been accomplished—
in spirit, in prayer, in joy,
through sexuality—
then there is nothing to separate.

A letter of farewell should be made legal
to protect those concerned.
It should be written with honor and kindness,
if possible with love.

But if spiritual love is present, then it is not good to divorce.
If sexuality alone is present without any soul contact,
then divorce is permitted and should even be encouraged.

Pray before a divorce happens.

The saint spoke again:

God created humanity, man and woman, male and female,
as a unity.
What God has brought together, let no one put asunder.
This belongs to the greater unity of all humankind.

Do not throw a stone at homosexuals.
But contemplate again and again
that God created human beings as man and woman,
and they are to remain in this unity!

Not just men, not just women make up creation,
but the whole human being, the maleness and femaleness,
of man and woman together.
This unity must not be put asunder.

13.6.1990
A saint spoke:

It is out of balance when human beings live divided—
men in the world of men's spirit,
women in the world of women's spirit.

An angel said:

The woman is a protector;
she loves all and cares for everything in daily life.
It is in her nature to pass on life and not to procure abortion.
It also lies within her nature
to pass on the life of Christ in the Eucharist—
as a priest or intercessor.

At the beginning of human existence,
when males contemplated the vast spaces on earth
without human beings
they desired to pass on life.
When they draw nearer to loving the protection of life
they do not need to make war.

The human being who passes on life in manifold forms—
as man or woman, a doctor, a sower of seeds or a priest—
lives the unity of man and woman.

February 1995
*Some years later friends of mine, who had just read these visions on the
metaphysical unity of male and female were concerned about the implication of this for homosexuals. They asked the following question: Is it
possible for men and women with homosexual inclinations to attain to
the inner unity of man and woman and experience human wholeness
on a psychological level? Together we went to church and, after we had
prayed, Luke the Evangelist appeared to me and answered:*

Listen!
Peter, Paul and others were married.
John the Evangelist bore within himself
deep spiritual love for a woman.

For Christ, every human being was
a being of soul, spirit, and light.
I, Luke, loved my wife.
Even in our times there was homosexuality.
Christ did not throw a stone at them.
He saw their soul, spirit, and light.
Your friend is right.
In order to become whole in one's own self
it is possible to unite male and female inwardly.
There are many ways of achieving this,
for example, through a powerful experience
that shocks one into a new realization
or through encounters with other human beings.
It often happens through discussions
with psychologists, theologians, or medical doctors.
Reflect on all this.

3.6.1992
*I was in the church, and I asked about a particular relationship between
a man and woman whom I knew. A saint answered:*

A serious and solid connection has grown between them—
the spiritual unity of man and woman.

Luke the Evangelist added:

This kind of union of soul and spirit
between man and woman is not dissolvable.
It survives in the hereafter as a spiritual force.
There, where there is neither man nor woman
but only beings of light,
the created force of the union created between man and woman
nevertheless remains present.

With Jesus, this particular kind of union was not present.
Spiritually, he lived and loved the wholeness of human beings.
He loved men and women equally.
He loved his mother and the women disciples.
He did not live and work only with men.

The first to meet him after his death was a woman.
Not a trace of separateness or disparity!
The union of soul and spirit, male and female,
brings forth the great power of light
inherent in human nature.
Write all this down!

*I asked Luke if the power of light with this particular man and woman
can be attained in union with more than one person. Can it be attained
more than once? Luke answered:*

There are many relationships and friendships.
They may be good, blessed, or even holy.
But there is only one great power of light.
One great love: one new birth.
Do not ask further.
Do not be afraid to pass on these words.

17.3.1993
A woman artist had a question about love. Francis of Assisi spoke:

You know that this woman is God-fearing
and therefore seeks what is most exalted, powerful,
and pure in life.
Her searching in art,
her searching for the unity of man and woman,
is all part of this.
She seeks the physical unity between man and woman.
This is good.
Nevertheless, spiritual wholeness in the unity of man and woman
is far greater.

Slowly:

She will find it and be happy.
Amen.

Eusebia, a saint of ancient Rome, added:

Let this woman affirm her sexuality
and love the sexuality of the man.

May she develop courage to touch his body,
be at one with him, and yet remain free and true to herself.
It is important that she works on this.

*A young woman asked me if she could marry a man who was training
to become a priest in the Serbian Orthodox Church. I brought this
question before the altar. Mary answered:*

A marriage with a priest, of any confession,
must be done with complete love—
that means with love for God and for one's fellow human being.
This love must come from both persons.

28.5.1983
A saint continued to speak about man and woman:

A spiritual woman of high degree
and a spiritual man of high degree,
each with their own personal soul and spirit,
are together a sphere of light.
In their living together, through their spiritual life and work,
they constitute not only a physical unity,
but the human being created in God's likeness!

What God has brought together, let no one put asunder.
These words are deeper and greater
than you have yet understood today.
Men only, women only: That is not God's creation!
Together the earth is subject to them—
to the spirit, soul, and body of the human being.
This unity forms the human being in God's image and likeness.

Royal is the woman.
Royal is the man.

There are great tasks for man and woman!
The responsibilities and the types of work
are to be divided among them—
in accord with the order of creation,

whether in the study of medicine or theology.
Women are very well suited to participate in the priesthood.

It is good if children have both men and women as teachers.
In this way a child will be educated holistically.

A saint spoke to me about this theme:

God created man and woman as a whole,
like two halves of a circle.
This whole does not bear only offspring,
but the spiritual evolution of future generations.
A life together in this unity
is more than a life as a separate individual.

The encounter with the opposite sex stimulates hormones
and creates life energy.
There are many ways of creating life energy—
through joy, dance, and music.
The release of hormonal energy can happen up to old age
through contact, whether physical or spiritual,
with men and women who remain alive and full of energy.

– 9 –

Patterns of Nature, Patterns of the Spirit

The visions now open us up to the world of informative patterns. They appear to be coded patterns that inform the entirety of creation on different levels. In animals and humans, they approximate to what have been otherwise termed "inherited modes of functioning," "core schemata," "archetypal propensities," "providential callings." Informative patterns are alive because they come from the source of life. Informative patterns have existed since the beginning of evolution. They are part of our ancestral heritage. They already influence us when we are in the womb, and later we can experience them in a personal way. Great care is needed in nourishing the rich potential of informative patterns, which are crucial to the development of soul and spirit in first seven years of a child's life. Informative patterns vary from people to people. The visions in this section emphasize that through music, prayer, and relationship to God, further patterns of information may be assimilated, bringing new life, healing, and wholeness, bringing us one step further toward eternal life.

A Risen One, brown-skinned, perhaps from India, spoke:

It is important to identify the informative patterns
that have been given to humankind.
There are informative patterns that have come from the Source,
and have been present since the beginning of human evolution.
Others have been received by the ancestors
and can be inherited.
There are also informative patterns from the time in the womb,
and others from birth onward.
These are our own experiences.
It is important to know this for psychology.

Informative patterns already given to the first human beings.
The patterns for the peoples of the East,
the West, the North, and the South are different.
The inheritance of Africans
differs from the inheritance of Europeans.
There are specific informative patterns for the different peoples.
They can be inherited directly from ancestors,
even bypassing several generations.
Remember, there are patterns received
during the time in the womb;
But there are also patterns derived
from individual experience after birth.

Eusebia added:

The informative patterns that human beings receive
are very important for their becoming.
The development of human beings
comes into being with the development of the cells
of the cerebrum and the cerebellum.

Later, while in prayer, I was told:

Whenever a person lives truly and authentically,
in the Christian way of life, and has light within,
coded patterns flow from this person to all living creation.

A Risen One spoke:

You will understand it soon.
It is the life of creation.
I want to emphasize informative patterns
from the sun, rain, climate, radiations, or music,
which penetrate trees and stones.
These kinds of patterns belong to the life of creation.
If a tree is dead, it no longer absorbs any of these impulses.

*I asked, how are informative patterns given? Do they come to us
through the spirit or through natural law? Are they delivered by the
winds? I don't understand these patterns.*

Listen! The next stage is to understand
life in the cosmos and on earth and what it means for humans!
Informative patterns are part of creation.
In the first place they can be given spiritually,
from God and Christ through the Holy Spirit.
They are there for us to assimilate through prayer.
They can also come from the sun, the wind, and the water.
They really do reach you!

The Risen One spoke again:

God, Spirit, light, energy:
these are the origin of creation!
That is what life is about!

Again Eusebia spoke:

Informative patterns have been inherited from earlier periods
and still exist in humans today.
They can be lost
through disease or trauma.

*I asked: If this loss happens through a shock, then can the same happen
through sin? Does sin change the cells? The saint answered:*

Yes.

An angel explained to me:

Inherited patterns do not come from reincarnation.
It is good to work through inheritances,
with the guidance Christ brought us,
until shadows over one's spiritual life give way
and all is in light.

Later another risen person spoke:

Human cultures and developments arise
through patterns, impulses.
The school of faith, however, requires human endeavor.
Look at early Christian Ireland.
This is the process of God's relationship to humanity.
Vibrations reach Christ and God
through prayer and the sacraments.
Then informative patterns descend from God to the human cells.
Humans are transformed—they develop—
and sick cells can be healthy again.
This can happen to the trees and animals too,
through prayer.
The animals, trees, and plants absorb the impulses
from the informative patterns.
The impulses reach them from outside.
Hence human beings with their spirit
can pass on these patterns through Christ and God.

Once, after having prayed, I thought about a lecture on the dying trees. Apparently forest wardens search for the seeds of old, healthy Alpine trees. They call them "grandmother trees." These trees have absorbed informative patterns from their surrounding environment over a long period of time. These impulses come from the sun, winds, rain, snow, cold, and heat, so that the developing cells acquire the characteristics of an Alpine tree. When these cells are ill, as they are now with endangered forests, it can take fifty years for new Alpine trees to be cultivated—for a valley pine to become a mountain pine.

A saint continued to speak about this theme:

Cell patterns can heal pain,
be it personal or among a people, animals, or plants.
This even happens in the case of informative patterns for the cell
that come from Christ and God—even without prayer.
If you suffer for the people of Israel and walk by their side
on the path of distress, you will take their pain away,
not all the pain, not all the suffering,
but you will participate and help them.
This happens through compassion.
Help Israel and accompany it on its path from time to time.
Do you understand this? Ripen! Grow!
Compassion has nothing to do with moaning and groaning.
Don't moan or groan!
Accompany them and share their burden
before God and with God.

I thought about all this. An angel then stood before me and said:

Through the intervention of the spirit,
informative patterns pass even to the cells of other human beings
and change them.

Mary spoke:

A person of spirit is formed through a process of becoming.
When humans lived in nature,
they sensed the life of the spirit in and around them.
The development of soul and spirit began

when coded patterns came to human beings from God
and through heredity. This is still happening today.
A corpse no longer absorbs these patterns.
Informative patterns are life.

– 10 –
How Informative Patterns Function

A saint said:

Listen! All human beings contain musical patterns
from their homeland, the land of their origins.
Therefore it is important that even sick people
from time to time
listen spiritually and bodily to the music of their homeland.
A Greek should hear Greek music.
An Israeli should hear Israeli music.
A Scandinavian should hear Scandinavian music.
An Italian should hear Italian music.
An Irish person should hear Irish music.
An African should hear African music.
Think about the Mexicans, Austrians,
Swiss, Germans, and others.
Don't forget to reveal these words!
There are rhythmic vibrations that pass
through the soul, the spirit, and the body.

*A further example of how informative patterns function was given
to me in words about Noirin Ni Riain, the well-known Irish singer.
Noirin once told me that she had to sing the way her Celtic soul dictated.
I prayed about this and an answer came in the following words:*

Noirin's singing embodies a transmission of the spirit
by means of heredity
from the period of 550 to 670 and 730 C.E.!

Informative patterns have also come to her since birth,
and through her natural development in life.
Thus she has acquired the typical features
of a singer of Celtic Christian songs.
Learn from this.

*I once asked about a Japanese medical doctor who was in a process of
soul-searching. A saint answered:*

It is important for this Japanese doctor to wander
through China and Mongolia.
There he should breathe in the scents
of the plants, grass, and trees,
observe the light over the land, and hear the people speaking.
In this way he will become peaceful, confident, and creative.
His soul will be healed.

*Perhaps this vision is connected to the fact that the ancestors of the
Japanese people came from China and Mongolia. Another saint spoke
in answer to my question about a musician in Australia:*

She should walk through the bush lands.
She should then meditate on the ancient period of life
of the Aborigines in Australia.
Once she has assimilated their informative patterns,
she should read your visions,
especially the part on the ten messages of wisdom.
Since she has already experienced
the history of the Irish church in depth,
she can weigh, as with a scale,
the light from the old Celtic church
and the patterns received from Aboriginal Australia.
A new understanding and new life will grow from all this.

– 11 –
Cell Membranes

An angel spoke:

New cell membranes are created for human beings
so that they can experience the radiance
of God's light through Christ
and the activity of the Holy Spirit.
New cell membranes are created for human beings
to evolve toward integration of the primal laws of creation,
in spirit and body—in a truly human way.
Thus their being can be authentic before God
and authentic in their way of loving!
Write this down; it is a very important part of creation.

Later an angel explained to me:

The human being can assimilate more informative patterns
through this creation of new cell membranes.
Active, creative individuals have more of these cell membranes.

*An angel added that these cell membranes are not inherited, but are
a new creation for each human being. I understood that these cell
membranes are not the same as those described by biologists.*

– 12 –
Soul and Spirit

*While I was writing this book, a man in his early twenties spoke to
me about a problem he was experiencing. As soon as there was sexual
contact between himself and the woman he loved, he became afraid
and began to stutter. He asked me why this happened and what its*

cause could be. *We discussed various matters that could be related to his speech defect. He had already had a number of sexual relations but never had this problem. I promised to telephone him, if I received an answer.*

I prayed for the young man and did receive a response. In prayer, I was shown the period when he was in his mother's womb. I was reminded about his mother's wanting to put an end to the pregnancy. She had received approval from the state psychiatrist. However, I knew the mother finally decided against having an abortion and thus he was born.

In vision I was shown what really happened. This little being still in the womb could only love his mother. His entire trust and growth were fused with her! From this deep source of unity, security, and love also came the possibility of being destroyed by his mother. I was shown that when this man is involved in a deep love relationship, and it does not have to be sexual, the fear of being destroyed returns, manifesting in a stutter. In vision it was said that this is an example of depth psychology.

Later I asked him if he knew about the possible abortion and he answered yes. I promised him we would try to work on this and bring healing.

Eusebia spoke in the presence of Mary, the mother of the Lord:

The coming into being of a new soul and new spirit
begins at conception.
When all the cell patterns for a human being are present
in the union of semen and ovum,
then the development of a new soul and spirit begins.
Hold on to this! Amen.

A Risen One spoke:

The cultivation of the soul begins at birth.
The soul receives signals through the brain.
Informative patterns are given to skin, the ears, the eyes,
to all the sense organs.
A human being can be born in poverty
and yet receive great wealth for his soul

from his surroundings—
physical warmth, love, security,
the comforting voices of men, women, and children,
the sounds of animals, the rustle of the wind,
the movement of the plants.
Truth is a pillar of support for the growth of the soul and spirit.
Truth makes the individual strong and secure,
gives him or her the basic values of life
in order to become independently active.
The link to God, first given by the mother and father,
is important.[1]
This link provides the true spiritual foundation for a human life.
An education that brings recognition of authentic values
in the first seven years of a child's life
is crucial for the whole life of that human being.

– 13 –

Children in Different Cultures

*My dead grandmother from Sweden explained to me how the women
of Lapland educate their children:*

A child in Lapland stays with its mother
for five months after birth.
After the fifth month, the parents share the responsibility
for the child's life with the community.
After the sixth or seventh year, the child learns to be self-confident
in many areas of life. It is important to know this.
As a result, the mother gains more free time.
The children are less afraid, and grow
into self-confident individuals
of the strong, quiet, northerly type.

---

1. The parents can use stories and common prayers.

In Africa, children remain only with the mother and grandmother,
and develop to become the gentle, peaceful type.
The children of Mexico and South America hear a lot of music!
These children become cheerful through rhythm and movement.
The most important task for parents and environment
in the first seven years of a child's life
is to help develop the brain.
The brain develops as the individual becomes conscious of life.
By the seventh year, a child must be secure in its will
and confident in its ability to act in life.
The learning of different languages, musical skills,
and all that is developed by the use of the intellect
can be accomplished more easily after the seventh year
if this core development has been successful.
This is a developmental pattern!

Peter, my son, who has risen from the dead, added:

What you, my parents, have given to us, your children,
is a sense of responsibility toward all of life,
toward all forms of life in the order of creation:
God and God's creation, our fellow human beings,
the animals, and all created things.
Thus there was formed in me a love, a fundamental love,
rooted in my spirit,
that counts far more than all the knowledge of the world.
If this kind of love is in the human soul,
we, the saints and angels, can help.
When love is not there, a shadow is cast upon the soul,
which we, the resurrected, cannot change.
These are primal laws.

Later a Risen One spoke:

Let us continue.
In the search for truth, we find signs that are contradictory.
You understand evolution and the unfolding of spirit
to be the same. There is a difference.
On the one hand plants, animals, and human beings

participate in evolution. Evolution is the work of creation.
On the other hand, an unfolding of spirit happens
with God's grace and light.
It is consummated only in what is of the image
and likeness of God—the human being.
The unfolding of spirit happens over thousands of years!
Let humans come into their existence
through the development of spiritual understanding.
Evolution can be hectic; the unfolding of the spirit is timeless.

– 14 –

Dreams

Life on earth is deepened, becomes more authentic, and can be celebrated through the understanding of dreams and through color, form, rhythm, and dance. According to these visions, dreams, given to us by God since the beginning of time, influenced important stages of the soul's evolution. Linking the past and future, ancestor and child, they helped men and women develop a consciousness of continuity and identity. Dreams continue to reveal the soul's informative patterns, bringing messages from the source of life. They are designed by God to give us greater knowledge of soul and spirit. The task of a person working with dreams is not only to bring understanding, but also healing, meaning, and a linking with God's light. Joa's visions exhort us not to be afraid, but to have confidence in life. We must love and seek to express its fullness in sound, color, form, and body movement. Saying yes to life in all its manifestations on earth renders visible the human in the image and likeness of God and prepares us for our greater life in heaven.

An angel spoke:

Let us begin with dreams.
Dreams are informative patterns—to a person's soul and spirit.

Soul and spirit in turn pass on this information to the brain.
Events in dreams can correspond to reality,
or their meanings can be concealed,
for instance by the use of symbols.
They may bring us a message
or prepare us for something.
Since the beginning of our creation and existence on earth,
dreams have made it possible for us to receive informative patterns
from the world of the spirit.
Whoever can assimilate and understand these messages
will possess a greater knowledge of the spirit.

There are also dreams that arise from daytime experiences,
which may have a positive or a negative effect on the dreamer.
When negative experiences are not worked through,
with the help of discussion, prayer, or meditation,
they remain imprisoned in the soul and cast a shadow on life.
One of the great discoveries of C. G. Jung
was to identify and analyze such dreams
that contain informative patterns still imprisoned in the soul
and thus bring healing. A difficult endeavor.

It is right and important that the analysis be linked
to a relationship with Christ.
Thus the sick parts of the soul that have been identified
can be healed through prayer and light—with God's help.
Therefore don't just disentangle, decipher, and clarify,
but heal and make healthy!

The angel continued:

Angels mentioned in the Old and New Testaments
conveyed messages through dreams.
God has created dreams
to help human beings since the beginning of human existence.

A risen person spoke:

Dreams are an important stage in the evolution
of soul and spirit—important for

the I-Thou relationship and for the relationship
to the whole of being.
Dreams also provide a better understanding
of the connection between the self and the ancestors
and what is to become.
There are only a few people who find
the deeper connections to their ancestors
and other human beings in a waking state.
Early humankind developed a consciousness
of what their ancestors—
of what their father, mother, child, and others—
meant through dreams.
Individual dreamers developed a consciousness of community
through their spiritual connection to the past
through their ancestors,
as well as to the future through their children,
and to their fellow humans.
Dreams gave the gift of continuity
and a consciousness of community
and thus furthered the future unfolding of human life on earth.

*There are many kinds of dreams. An angel mentioned three ways they
can meet us:*

Dreams can work in different ways—
as "wake-up calls"; as "residue processing";
and as "messages."

The "wake-up" aspect arouses the conscious mind
of the individual,
so as to restore order or to encourage reflection
on some matter.
Dreams that shock the individual can do the same.
The "residue dreams" are reflexes from the previous day,
often appearing after films or discussions.
They have no meaning
other than to help process such experiences.
The "message" aspect brings direction and guidance for life.

Messages can also be experienced in prayer and visions.
However, this visionary capacity has become extinguished
in seventy percent of humanity.
Even when a dream message has not been understood,
nevertheless an indication remains
that one should pray for the content of the dream!
To integrate messages from dreams in prayer
is important!
That means, asking God—through Jesus Christ—
to help and be active with light,
and to intervene through the Holy Spirit.

In this way the dream will become spiritually alive.
To integrate dreams in one's spiritual life is authentic;
it accords with the truth of creation and the Christian way.

A Risen One said:

The language of images is the living language of the soul
often expressed by symbols, especially in dreams.

*I once dreamt of many empty houses. Many people, sometimes without
eyes, wandered away from them. I asked the heavens about this dream.
An angel answered:*

It foretells the coming migrations of people
who are without spiritual guidance.

*I understood this to refer to wars and refugees. Therefore I began
to pray.*

An angel once instructed me to write a letter:

Write to A. and tell her that there are important differences
in the way a person receives messages.
Prophecy, given by God, is the highest kind of message.
Clairvoyance is a gift,
but has nothing to do with direct messages from God.
Clairvoyance is one expression of a primal sensitivity.
Recognize the dreams sent by God.
They contain messages from God,

as for example, Joseph's dreams in the New Testament.
The naturally occurring spiritual phenomena
of strange figures, otherworldly music, or mysterious images
emanate from within the human spirit.
The spirit is alive, active, and radiating.
Put your soul and your spiritual life in order,
and your work in this area will become clearer.

– 15 –
Dreams and Their Origins

An angel explained to me:

Know the difference:
— the development in the womb endows the child
with the capacity to respond with a healthy nervous system;
— the first eight months of a child's life after birth
can be responsible for impaired behavior
over a whole lifetime!

Dreams can arise from the time in the womb
or from the first eight months after birth,
from healthy responses or from early wounding.
A supportive behavior toward the child, however,
should not be limited to those eight months.
Human growth and development continue until old age!

The angel continued:

Dreams are signs of the spirit and soul.
Dreams of the spirit express perceptions
from a person's whole lifetime.
Dreams of the spirit also express a receptivity
to communications beyond one's earthly life.

Such are Joseph's dreams in the Old Testament
and St. Joseph's in the New Testament.
Those who have been trained in matters of the spirit
and have achieved spiritual maturity
receive these kinds of dreams often.
People who cannot hear or see in visions
but who can understand and interpret what is given to them,
do receive such dreams of the spirit.

An angel spoke about symbols:

Symbolic images from dreams
are to be found in the Old Testament!
Laws of the spirit arose from the ways of living then.
These were, are, and will remain.
A person who bows before another
expresses humility.
This is an example.

A human being who is earnest, spiritually open,
and wants to grow
will receive answers in dreams.
To interpret these answers requires wisdom.
A wise man or woman is capable
of receiving and understanding messages of the spirit.
It is important that such people of wisdom forget themselves.
Then God's light and the spirit of God's creation
can be active in them.

*A relative of mine often had powerful dreams. I once told her that I
always had to verify in prayer what I received in visions, and maybe
she should do the same with her dreams. She asked me how could she
do that? I prayed and an answer came from St. Luke:*

There are many dream symbols.
When your relative can't understand them,
she should speak with a psychologist
who understands and respects the Christian faith.

Or she should try in prayer to say:
"I have received this dream. I do not understand it.
I place its meaning in the light of Christ
and let myself be guided by the Holy Spirit."
You can search for the meaning of some dreams through prayer.
The symbolic language of dreams goes back
over thousands of years.
To understand certain important dreams
you might need a trained psychologist—one who is schooled.

– 16 –

Examples of Dreams and Their Meanings

*A woman known to me, the mother of two children, once telephoned.
She had received an impossible dream and did not dare to tell anybody,
not even her psychologist. She then described the dream to me: I was
a man, and a man in every possible way. I was only missing a beard.
I was carrying a flower. What I found weird was that it was not
so very different from being a woman. After she told me her dream,
I comforted her and assured her that there are many books about this
kind of dream. In the evening, as I was in prayer, I asked if this dream
had any significance for the woman. Why did she dream it? After all,
she does not want to be a man. The answer was:*

She received this dream to help her recognize
that there are commonalities between men and women.
By means of the dream, she began to overcome her fear of men.
A man became for her a human being.

*I understood this dream to mean that this woman must recognize the
common humanity shared by men and women. Through her recognition
of what is shared she will overcome her fear.*

I asked, Why the flower? The answer was:

She never lost the enjoyment of her sexuality,
despite her fear of men.

Another woman who was planning to become a Buddhist nun dreamt about a snake with a swan's head. Mary Magdalene spoke about this symbol:

Overcome the snake with prayer.
Let the swan's head live.
The snake is her searching and struggling.
The swan's head on the snake
is what she has experienced consciously.
Let her have this consciousness
until she wants to take the next step.

I learned from these words the important lesson that this woman should continue her journey in her own way.

I would like to present a dream of my own. In this dream I saw my father, who had been a traveling salesman, riding in a train. He died many years ago. An angel explained:

A train—that's life.
Your father is "active" and has a "job" to fulfill
before God.
Through the dream you can share in his work
by knowing about it.
That means your father fulfills his task
in and with the light of Christ.

– 17 –
Art in the Fullness of Life

Mary, the mother of the Lord, spoke to me:

Living in the fullness of life on earth is most essential.
In order to do this, confidence and trust in life are necessary.
Whoever has confidence and trust
in creation (*the cosmos*), God (*religion*), and the earth (*humanity*),
and whoever has love within is not afraid.

Love of music and rhythm is part of this.
Love of color—that is important too.
To say "yes" to color means saying "yes" to an inner life.
This brings confidence and security.
Affirmation, assent, "yes" to life, trust in the powers of healing,
joy in the sun, and in the movements and warmth of the body.
These are important.

Mary again spoke to me:

Reflect about this:
The essence of humanity is in the Johannine message!
All of life is contained in it!

– 18 –
Colors: The Stations of the Cross

A close friend of mine who is an artist wanted to paint the Stations of the Cross. We spoke about the colors. She wanted to paint the stations without form, just with color. In vision a risen Russian saint, who was a painter of icons, appeared to me ready to give advice to this artist. He began to speak:

May the artist pray before she creates each station.
A cry of anguish is to be painted brown to black.
Light gray, light blue are to be the colors of the Holy Spirit.
Pain is dark red.
Energy, life, strength, and help can be expressed
with the colors yellow to orange.
Death is represented by black.

Colors are sources of energy.
They work according to their differences.
Before the deaths of the Kennedy brothers,
you saw angels shining in red,
symbolizing suffering and death.
You have often seen Mary in a blue light.
This blue symbolizes a protective light.
No blue light, not even with Mary,
was present at the way of the cross.
It was not even present as she stood under the cross.
At that moment she did not receive a protective light from God!
You have never seen blue light with Christ,
but you have seen his radiance in different shades of yellow.
God gave the plants of the earth
the radiance of yellow and blue together—green!

I asked about the brown earth. The saint answered:

The color brown, which belongs to the way of the cross,
is a cry of anguish.
The brown of the earth refers to the cycles
of becoming and decaying
that have always been part of creation.

Suddenly another risen person stood in front of me and said:

I am Meister Eckhart. Listen!
The stations of the cross bear meaning for the spirit,
similar to the passion of Christ, as painted in icons.
There are different ways to experience Christ's passion—
word, color, form.

It is important that a true sensitivity
be released in all who contemplate the Passion.
The color, form, and brushstrokes
must elicit the enormous pain of this event.
For example:
sand beside water in a painting
can bring forth sadness and tears.

May your close friend wash her hands
before she works on the paintings.
Let her make the sign of the cross
on her forehead and on her feet.
Then she can begin, slowly and inwardly, to work.
This is a ritual.
I, Eckhart, saw that she will be guided
and will create a great work of art.

– 19 –
Dance Therapy

*In one of my visions, a famous psychologist, now risen from the dead,
spoke about dance therapy:*

You have it!
A spiritual experience, a release of movement—this is right!
Body movement as therapy should work together
with the life of the spirit.
For example, experiences through dance, music,
the telling or enacting of fairy tales, theater, and discussions
can bring joy.
Such experiences influence and release body movement.
They can loosen cramped limbs.
Likewise negative experiences can bring new tensions in the body.
Observe life.

Spiritual experiences influence the nerves and muscles.
The task of a therapist is to evaluate such experiences
in a helpful way.
Also, words of the therapist such as,
"Today we will try to loosen tension in the hands
through movement."
This activates and brings movement to the spirit.

– 20 –

The First Cultural Signs of Humanity

In vision, these signs were shown to be the signs of the aboriginal people of Australia.

With fingers and hands in the earth—a circle.
With hands and fingers—a roof, hovering above the earth.
A square.
A square, small lines pointing inwards.

A square with a circle. Later small spirals,
moving counterclockwise, between circle and square.

The circle remained empty for a long time.
Later came the path toward the center.

– 21 –

Psychology and Religion: Trust in Life and the Source of Life

Finally, the visions in this part of the book warn us about the spiritual crisis of the present time. Humans have lost their trust in life, having been subject to countless ideologies that have robbed them of their dignity and freedom. A traditional approach in religion, science, politics, and other aspects of cultural life, can no longer be unquestionably affirmed or believed. Individuals are obliged to make their own meaning in these areas of experience. The task of the psychologist is to restore trust in life, and the task of the theologian is to restore relationship to the source of life. We are called to put on a new garment, a simple honest garment expressing genuine love and care. It is a garment of the spirit, yet visible to the world, and, we might assume, is visible in a continuous universe after we have completed our life on earth.

A saint spoke:

First, become truly human, then understand psychology,
and then take in religious understanding.
These are the three stages.

A close friend, a psychologist, put forward a question. A saint answered:

Warn your friend, the psychologist!
With psychology, you can reach into the depth of the soul
without bringing light from the Source, from God!
This can lead to disintegration of the spirit.
This is law.
Primal energy must be present—
then you have the possibility of development.
Your friend is to continue his work in psychology.

He should maintain his link with God,
and pass on light to others.

The saint continued:

The purpose of psychology
is to seek, to study, and to repair
those areas in the human being
where there is no trust.
Then the psychologist must help those who have been healed
to find meaning in their lives!
The Christian religion provides the supreme meaning of life:
the receiving and giving of light, love, and justice.

*I once asked about the difference between the tasks of a psychologist and
a theologian. Mary, the mother of the Lord, spoke:*

Learn from this!
Those who live without a higher authority,
that is, with their whole being turned toward the earth
and without a link to God,
may live from what they hear, from hearing and seeing—
from literature, art, and nature.
They live powerfully connected with the earth,
with its evolution and history.
But whoever sees and hears the earth in its entirety,
the planets, the sun, and the stars, *lives from the spirit,*
from the energies of creation,
and the rays of primal light.
If such people become tired
and their soul loses balance,
anarchy and chaos may gain strength over them.
Where such chaos reigns,
the psychologist, the interpreter of dreams,
is there to help people.
The theologian's task is to work for the spiritual link
between God and humans.
Many are connected to Christ, the Holy Spirit,
and the Father of all creation in such purity

that they do not need a theologian,
only the "rock" as a shelter, a place to pray,
praise, give thanks, and participate communally
in the Lord's Supper.

A risen person then spoke further about this theme:

Psychology and religion form a large area of the human spirit.
Soul and spirit are to be understood and ordered
so that we can work with them.
It is a task that can hardly be completed, but an urgent one.
For many people this is the only way to find Christ authentically.
Not just theology, but psychology and theology together
bring healing to humanity.
To perceive consciously the state of the psyche, to explain it,
and then to expand on it with religion
requires courage and deep knowledge
of religion and psychology.

Later another risen person added:

Seeing and understanding creates community.
See your neighbor, meet him or her in a Christian way;
this creates community.

– 22 –
A Loss of Trust

Already in 1985 a saint spoke about loss or trust:

There was a crisis of trust during the Hitler period,
and again at the end of colonial rule,
particularly in those countries
that fell into the hands of the communists!

What used to be dependency in those countries
has now become slavery at its worst.
Human dignity has been taken away from the people.
Technology also brings about a loss of trust,
causing doubt and uncertainty
at the innermost levels of soul and spirit!
Help these people to find trust in life!

Individuals rejected the traditions
and began to study for themselves
in every area of human experience
—in religion, in medicine, in politics.
From the crisis of trust in the churches,
in psychology, medicine, politics,
and the world situation in general,
there followed a development
with enormous consequences
that has not yet come to an end.

The crisis in the churches
released great uncertainty and shock.
Have courage, put on a new garment.
Let it be of the spirit, yet visible to the world!
This new garment must not manifest
outdated ecclesiastical attitudes toward the people!
The new garment must be simple, expedient,
woven in the spirit of Christ.
In the presence of God and all humans,
you must be authentic, honest, kind-hearted,
and full of genuine love and care for others.

Part Two

ALIVE IN HEAVEN:
RISEN FROM
THE DEAD

Introduction

Having experienced the death and resurrection of her son in a very personal and intense way, some twenty years were to pass until they again became the focus of Joa Bolendas' visionary life. She told me that during those intervening years, the Risen Ones often spoke to her, informing and helping her to understand and express the messages of heaven. At that time she was glad not to have to handle the death and resurrection of individuals who were close to her. This might have been too powerful, too hard, and too soon after the experience of her son's death.

Focus on that great passage from death to the greater life, however, began again in 1985 and constitutes the main part of this book. In that year, she was already seventy years old and had been living in retirement with her husband in the Swiss Alps. Between 1985 and 1991, she received most of the visions contained here.

The Four Answers at the beginning of the section describe in a more general way how men and women receive light from God on earth and later in heaven. Through this light they pass through death and evolve toward the greater life, participating in eternal life in the image and likeness of God. The great task of religions on earth is to help individuals become God's people of light while alive on earth and later when they are alive in heaven.

According to these visions, risen life is not just a place to sit on a cloud, nor is it a gloomy place of mortification, as expressed in the countless works of theologians, poets, and artists. The resurrection of life, promised by Christ, begins shortly after death. Often the first words of the Risen Ones are: I am alive! They stand in sheer amazement before the continuity of their own existence. Then begins a path of development, on many different dimensions, not unlike one's actual or wished for development on earth. They seem to maintain the same character and interests as they had on earth. The risen Severino continues to be curious about natural science, although he never studied it. Franz Eibner discovers anew the wonder of music, his lifelong passion. The sculptor battles with his tough character, realizing how it hurt people when he was alive on earth. An unborn child continues to grow in heaven and wants her mother on earth to share precious moments with her. In these visions the continuity of character of the Risen Ones is as important as the information that they convey.

Here we encounter Risen Ones who look back on their life on earth, what it was, what it could have been. They meet their loved ones, particularly those who have passed on before them— their ancestors, their parents, their friends who also have changed in amazing and unexpected ways. They are helped by the saints and the angels and become aware of the presence of Christ or Mary. They talk about their work on earth, their interests, and their professions. They discuss all those dimensions of life that concern philosophy, music, psychology, or the natural sciences. Some witness the creation of a star, or the wondrous path of earth's evolution—the movement of creation from inorganic matter to the plant, to the animal, to the human being (see note, p. 172). Others visit sacred places that they longed to see when they lived on earth—Mount Sinai, the Wailing Wall, Bethlehem. The people of the Far East, according to Joa's visions, meet their ancestors, who guide them further on their way to enter the seemingly unending dimensions of God's world.

The deceased are instilled with the mighty power of God and, after a certain period of development, are given different tasks to accomplish. Many of these tasks are concerned with helping people on earth—working for peace, inspiring and guiding the teachers of religion, comforting the suffering and dying, protecting children, sharing their creative gifts with artists, musicians, and philosophers.

Some form of mortification does exist in the next world, but it does not appear as an unrestricted fantasy that vanquishes all others. In one vision, not published in this work, Joa Bolendas witnessed the sad fate of an individual who was partly responsible for some of the horrors of World War II. This person will continue to work on the great harm and suffering that was done during that time for many hundreds of years, so that the wrongdoing be atoned. Through the prayers of those alive on earth, the spiritual evolution of such individuals can be helped.

Preface
by Joa Bolendas

Since the beginning of time, humankind has searched for a meaning to life and with that the possibility of survival after death. We humans have always questioned what it really means to be risen from the dead. Here I pass on some answers received through visions.

Two modern scientists, Jean Charon and Teilhard de Chardin, have addressed the topic of life after death from their respective viewpoints. Both adopt a scientific approach to the question of the human soul and its survival after death. I cannot profess

to answer or even understand all the questions raised by these
scientists. I appreciated the fact that a natural scientist and an an-
thropologist have attempted to explain the spiritual dimensions of
the universe and the possibility of survival after death on a scientific basis. It is my hope that the answers received in the following
visions will further clarify questions about life beyond death and
the imperishability of the human soul.

The Four Answers

The First Answer

*What is the substance of one risen from the dead? This was my question,
and a saint answered:*

It is a substance of spiritual energy,
a substance of light, unchangeable light—
which is the same as energy.
The risen human remains a created being
linked with God's Spirit.

The flesh, the earthly covering and clothing, falls away.

You can say this in other words:
Within the earthly clothing made for all human beings
the soul and spirit of the human,
together with God's light,
come into existence, evolve and develop.

They develop into an image and likeness of God—
a human united with God's Spirit!

Don't you see that when the earthly clothing falls away,
the risen being lives on!

Risen humans exist according to the primal laws of
living, giving and receiving.

This means they live, they give of their love,
and they receive God's light and strength and the Holy Spirit,
as they did when they lived on earth.

The Second Answer

Speaking of the development of the human being of light, the saint said:

The semen is given to the ovum.
During the last months of pregnancy,
the vessel of the already existing soul forms itself.
The development of the human spirit
coincides with the growth of the brain.

All this was created by the primal source—
by God.

At birth the child, God's creation,
comes into contact with life on earth.

Once the human is born and lives the fullness of life
then his or her development into a being of light begins.
Thus body, soul, and spirit receive God's Spirit.

The image and likeness of God consists of
the human body, soul, and spirit,
completed with God's Spirit and light.

When the earthly clothing falls away,
eternal light in human form remains.

This body of light lives!
God's Spirit is in it.

The people of light are noble and fulfilled
when integrated into God's kingdom.

Those who do not develop on earth
into the image and likeness of God

will begin their evolution in the kingdom of heaven
as beings of weaker light.
Eventually they will develop their full radiance
and become people of light—
all according to God's primal law.

The Third Answer

Mary, the mother of the Lord, spoke:

The greatness of the Lord Jesus Christ is his light,
unchanging, eternal light—primal light.

At birth he received primal light.
When he was twelve years old, he received primal light.
At the baptism in the Jordan, he received primal light.
He received primal light
in order to live and work as the Son of God until his death.

The light that he received on earth, in his human life,
made him, Jesus Christ,
into the figure of light for this earth.
He is this figure of light through his death, as the Risen One,
and as the mediator between God and humankind.

Christ was brought forth from God's own being,
and God gave him to humankind (John 1:18).

Thus light came to the earth, to human beings—
light from God to humankind.

This is the greatness of the Lord!
Blessed be those who believe, love, and receive light.

*As an example of a human being risen from the dead, Mary then
showed me my son Peter, who died when he was twenty-three. She
said:*

Peter is a man of light.
He was surrounded by prayer
as he developed in his mother's womb and in his youth.

He loved God.
He was connected to Christ.
He is now a holy man of light linked with Christ.

Learn from this:
There is God, who is the primal source.
There is Christ, who was brought forth from God,
and who is called the Son of God
because the magnitude of light received by him from God
is the same as God's, the primal source!

The angels are created by God as beings of light—
not with the same light as humans.

Risen men and women are people of light
without the clothing of earth.
(*My son Peter was shown as an example.*)
Many people grow to become people of light
in the kingdom of heaven.
Their levels of being are different.

A very few become extinguished.
They burn into nothing.
That is real death.

I asked Mary: What are you, Mary, as one risen from the dead? She answered full of joy:

I am risen!
I may serve Jesus—
I was created to serve.

The Fourth Answer

Mary summarized:

The risen body is a spiritual substance of energy.
Men and women are born with body, soul and spirit.
They develop in order that they may be linked with God.
You call it religion and faith.

Light comes into existence
through contact with God and Christ.
This light in men and women is imperishable.

Thus the life of the new human in heaven
will be soul, spirit, and light.
The light of those risen from the dead has human form.
The earthly covering falls away at physical death.

Do you understand this?
Pass on life—eternal life—to others,
so that you all may move toward becoming people of light!

Hold on to this:
The new church, the unified church,
is all that makes men and women into people of light!
Holy Scripture, the truths of the Old and New Testaments
will remain.
The church that has grown and developed will remain.
Repentance and reconciliation, baptism and the Eucharistic meal,
will remain.

Love is the sign and testimony of the Christian faith.

To be left open
are the ways in which different types of people develop.
Love the men and women of the East,
the Eastern Orthodox church,
of the North, the Protestant church,
and of the South, the Catholic church.
Do not be small-minded; be open and generous!
By the sign of love you will recognize them!

The Risen Ones Speak

– 1 –
My Son Peter

If life has taken a dear one away from you, then you will know about the pain and sadness such a loss causes. When our twenty-three-year-old son died through an accident, I was overcome by a powerful and deep sadness. Our son Peter possessed so many talents. This sadness was so great that, when I finally saw him in vision as one risen from the dead, I could only say:

I am grateful that you live.
I am grateful that joy is within you.
I am grateful that you can serve God and Christ.
But...
you are no longer with us.
You have gone elsewhere;
we remain on earth.

Peter answered:

Mother...
I implore you,
don't stay waiting at my grave.
Love me,
move with me
into the experience of the greater life.

We will work together!

I said:

What will you and I do together?

He replied:

I will forewarn you of two earthquakes
that nobody on earth knows about.
Then you will understand that I live.

The two earthquakes happened. Since then many years have passed. I have written a great deal about my experiences with those risen from the dead. Many experiences of this kind were integrated into my work So That You May Be One, *which contains many messages from the risen saints. Here I have selected a variety of people who have spoken to me from heaven, because their statements differ from one another according to the way they lived on earth.*

– 2 –

An Angel Speaks
of a Suicide

A woman I knew suffered greatly because her husband had committed suicide. I saw that she needed comfort. I prayed and in vision an angel spoke to me of her situation. The angel did not support the suicide, but perceived the depths of my friend's grief at her husband's violent death. The angel's words were healing and helped my friend pray for her husband with hope.

Life continues.
When the earthly covering falls away,
even if through violence or suicide,

the life of the human being—
the being of light—remains,
different in every case.
The development of every risen human is different
depending on that person's earthly life and circumstances.
While this person—your husband—moves beyond
on his path of light,
it is good, right, and meaningful
that friends on earth pray for him,
especially at the Eucharist.

– 3 –
A Catholic Priest

A Catholic priest I knew died. Risen from the dead, he said to me in vision:

I have to grow and develop until I am in the purity of light.
Then I may work and serve the Johannine church on earth.
I rejoice!

– 4 –
A Dying Man

I was praying for a dying man and asked that he might die in the love and protection of Christ. A saint answered:

What can be forgiven is forgiven.
What can evolve in new ways will evolve.
Amen.

And an angel said:

Humans can pray for the dead.
The dead can only serve human beings
when they have fulfilled a necessary spiritual development.

– 5 –

Krystophas

*In vision, a Greek saint, with a name sounding like "Krystophas,"
explained to me:*

Saints in the hereafter are the risen men and women,
who no longer have shadows from their lives on earth.

When humans on earth turn toward the saints,
and are in prayer before God,
then Risen Ones can absorb light from Christ
and pass it on so that it shines on earth.
This is the work and help of the saints toward the earth.
It is part of their life, activity, and work in the great life of
        heaven!
Welcome the saints in the life of the faith.

An angel said:

The final great development of the human
is in the great life after death.

– 6 –
A Husband

A woman mourned the death of her husband. She asked me to pray and I received a simple, clear answer from her husband:

I live and angels surround me.
I am happy and am loved by Christ.
I will develop stage by stage.
Rejoice with me and don't let your spirit be blocked
from that day when I changed my clothing.
I am moving on a path of light.
I love the earth and its people.
After the lesser life comes the greater life!
Rejoice!

– 7 –
Severino

Severino was a painter and decorator, a man of Italian origin and one of my relatives. Some weeks before he died, Mary, the mother of Jesus, spoke:

Pray aloud: Praise be to God,
who guides and helps,
who quickens and revives!
"Death, where is thy sting?"

15.1.1987
Severino had a heart attack. A few days later, he died. On the day he died, I saw him raised up, risen from the dead, and on his path through the next world. He met many people he had known on earth.

*One of the most beautiful light figures that he met was his mother as
a young woman. Some days later, in vision, Severino spoke to me:*

Do you realize
how great and beautiful heaven is?
How rich it is spiritually?
I can only be amazed!

Mary, the mother of Jesus, added:

Rejoice and jubilate.
Severino is loved!

17.1.1987
I heard him speaking to himself:

There really are angels.
Joa Bolendas should have drawn more angels.
There are no leaves... no green leaves.
They are only on earth.
I must get used to that.

19.1.1987
*Today I saw him looking back over a part of his life. It was like looking
at a film. He said:*

All was well and good in the first six years of my life.
I give thanks!

In the seventh year of my life
something went wrong.
It could have been healed.
(*Severino had problems with his lungs.*)

When I was fourteen...
I did not mean to harm anyone!
It was just for fun!

When I was sixteen... Yes, that hurt me.
It was the biggest disappointment of my youth.
(*I do not know what he was referring to.*)
But then my life moved like a swift wind.

Highlights in my life were:
when I first saw my wife,
when I took my own children in my arms for the first time.

From then on I was happy,
even though I experienced obstacles at work.

20.1.1987
Today I saw him in a very beautiful heaven. He said:

I will remain here some time.
I will grow,
and my spirit will develop one step further.

It is very interesting
that the process of life does not stand still!

21.1.1987
I saw Severino meeting an old friend of his, who died some years ago.
They talked. At the end of their conversation, the friend said:

You will see
how important our wives were for us.
Then like me you will recognize
that the unity of man and woman
together makes up the whole human being.
Whoever does not marry,
or live in a community with men and women,
needs a strong link with God and God's kingdom.
This person needs a special link with Jesus Christ.
It doesn't always have to be marriage,
but there must be spiritual contact
with other human beings and with God.

24.1.1987
Severino spoke:

Love is what is greatest
in our spiritual and psychological lives.
I can understand this now.

On earth, I thought justice came first,
but it is love that comes first.

Thoughtfully:

Love that comes from God
to human beings
makes life worth living.
You see it most visibly
in creation.
You see it in human beings, in animals,
in flowers, in every blade of grass and stone.
Love brings completion to men and women.

25.1.1987

Tell my family not to grieve.
If they love me,
they must move with me as I develop further
and not remain in mourning.

That evening, as I was in prayer, he spoke again:

Today I freed three people I didn't know on earth
from hatred.
I did it with prayer before Christ.
Christ, angels, saints bring it about
through the power of the Holy Spirit.

28.1.1987
Severino was looking at the earth and the human beings upon it. He glanced at me and said:

Interesting.
Is this known to human beings, known to science?
Humans have vibrations—vibrating tissuelike membranes—
around their heads.
They look like light.
The vibrations are more intense on the top of the head,
whiter and less intense around the body.
These membranes—yes, they are membranes—absorb vibrations.

Beneath the feet is a strong magnetic energy.
This same energy, though weaker, is to be found in the armpit.

It seems that the animals don't have this light.
Nevertheless their shoulder blades emanate energy in a similar way.

Is that why humans are humans?
Is that why they are in the image and likeness of God?

Severino looked over the earth, over the different countries. He looked at certain areas and saw differences in the membranes, according to the different peoples and their cultures. He saw that all human beings had these membranes.

2.2.1987
Severino prayed:

The pine trees are dying.
Many trees are ill.
Fish are dying; birds are dying.
The sands change their color to red and yellow.
Therefore we pray:

Father, forgive us.
We have sinned.
It is through our fault—our great fault.
May the winds turn.
May the sun rule over its light,
May the sun not darken.
Hold back the waters.
Save the climate!
Prevent explosion from within the earth.
Lord,
we ask you to have mercy.
Amen.

4.2.1987
Severino, looking toward the Vatican and wondering:

Much is no longer in balance in the church.
What do the cardinals of Rome really believe in?

They live for their positions!
Rome alone needs twenty Francises of Assisi!

The heart of the present pope is good,
but ambition and power are near to him.
That would be a pity for him.
I am amazed at what I see on earth.

Suddenly he looked to me and said:

Stand firm!
Hold on to all that you have received in vision. Don't retreat!

Then, looking back to the Vatican:

There, beside the Vatican, is Mary, the mother of Jesus.
She is joyful but looks out seriously
over the houses of the Vatican.
Wait. She said something to me.
Listen!

"Love them, they are servants.
Forgive them.
Pray for them."

"Forgive them.
You have experienced only a part of the church.
You have not experienced the church in all its fullness!"
(*Severino was a Roman Catholic when on earth.*)

"Your grandchildren and the next generation
will grasp what the church will be.
And you, Severino, will be permitted to see this.
Amen."

7.2.1987
*Today I asked Severino what will happen to a sick relative from
Ireland. He smiled and answered:*

I know where she is going to go.
She will rejoice!

9.2.1987
I asked Severino to forgive us, my family and me, because we had not yet visited his grave. He answered:

I am with you all.
Now and then I rejoice when my earthly remains are honored.
But I am with you,
wherever you may be.

10.2.1987
Today he spoke about the life of several risen human beings:

Your son is a great saint.

My mother is like a mother of light
for small children on earth who have been injured.
I don't know where and with whom my father can serve,
but there is light in the place where he is.

Your mother is a figure of light for Sweden,
for the older children.

Your father-in-law serves with musicians.

Hannes' father is now in heaven
and is helping the poor in a noble way.
(*Hannes is one of Severino's relatives.*)
He said that an angel from Mary
gave him a branch of a plant that always remains green.
The plant is called Love.

13.2.1987
Severino appeared and said:

I am beginning to learn how to love.

Next day he said:

I have been permitted to see
that many of God's messengers are close to Christ.
Also many saints are near to Christ.

There are angels with Mary.
Other angels, with a more intense light, are close to God.
Angels with colored rays of light—blue, red, yellow—
are with Christ.
You know them from your visions.

16.2.1987
He continued:

I have reached it,
the first phase of a process has been completed!

I live.
I love.
I am free from my earthly attitude to life.

Now there is peace.
Now I may begin to serve—
help children in Sicily, Uganda, Ethiopia.

17.2.1987
My son Peter spoke:

Severino has completed the first step in the greater life.

Now he is learning the second step:
contact with people on earth.
To receive light and impulses from Christ
is a process of learning.
To put to use these impulses
for the people on earth is new for Severino.

I too have learned many things.
To grasp the whole of creation
is to grasp an enormous and great diversity!

Severino added:

You should have seen that!
Beyond the heavens that are visible to you,
we saw how it roared and thundered in the universe.
It was more than a storm or hurricane.

It was as if everything in the universe was flying apart.
Does this belong to creation?
It was like the Big Bang.

22.2.1987
Severino:

I saw how Joseph and Mary appeared and spoke to you.
It was impressive.
Joseph, as a figure of light, has a powerful radiation,
He shines more powerfully than Abraham and Moses.

Three days later, Severino appeared again and said seriously:

Many children are crying.
My wife could do something to help them.
Here is a prayer for them:

From heaven come figures of light
to children who are sad and full of tears.
Let us give thanks to you, Jesus Christ,
who send these figures of light;
and we ask that the angels, the saints,
and the workings of the Holy Spirit
continue to meet these children.
Amen.

3.3.1987

Faith and love—
two mighty words.
Write down:
Faith in God and Jesus Christ
give great love and peace
to one's spiritual life.

Whoever knows and loves the truth of the faith
will reach the highest human development.
Therefore listen well:
to teach a person the faith
is a task and office of the highest nature.

A day later:

I have been allowed to help a thousand children.
I have been able to help stimulate their brains.

You don't believe it? Such things are possible
when you get to know the laws of creation.

4.3.1987
*Severino looked in the direction of the war between Iraq and Iran, and
exclaimed how horrible it was. With a loud voice he implored God:*

Please, O God, nothing more!

*He held out both his hands toward Iran to prevent a further expansion
of the war.*

6.3.1987
*Severino asked that we should give thanks for his death and resurrec-
tion with the following words:*

Father in heaven,
Jesus Christ,
praise and glory be to you.
For Severino could leave the earth, full of grace,
and now can live in the greater life, full of joy.
For the growth and development
he may experience in the kingdom of heaven,
let us praise, glorify, and thank God.
For all the work and help he may give
to the people and animals on this earth,
let us praise, glorify, and give thanks.
Praise be to God and Jesus Christ,
who love and help in this way!
Amen.

12.3.1987
Severino spoke again:

I saw Pilate in a Roman uniform,
with a lance in his hand.

He looked at me and said gruffly:
"I let him be killed!
We Romans killed him!
He died on the cross!"

After hearing these words, I saw Andrew, the brother of the apostle Peter. He said:

I loved him—
Jesus who was crucified.
We loved him
and were full of sadness and pain
when he was condemned to death on the cross—
when he was executed.
He suffered the terrible death on the cross,
until soul and spirit freed themselves from his body.

The body was buried, wrapped in cloths.
A round stone sealed his grave.
Jesus lived wholly in "the world of light" in the grave.

He, Jesus, appeared as a man of light with soul and spirit
to Mary Magdalene, to the other women and disciples.

As a man of light, he went through walls, and could even eat.
This to be understood metaphysically.

Metaphysically, a risen human being can appear
as a body of light—as a person of light—
similar to the way Jesus appeared to the two disciples of Emmaus.

I asked Andrew to tell me if the risen human is a person of light, containing soul, spirit, and God's Spirit in a human form full of light. Andrew answered:

Yes, that's right.

I asked further if a man or woman of light can really speak, sing, and be spiritually independent. Andrew said:

They can speak;
they can sing;

they can think in an independent way,
according to their level of development.
You have seen this with Severino the painter.
When he works for creation,
for the cosmos, for the planet earth,
for the people, animals, or plants,
he serves creation in a true and authentic way,
serves God and Christ.

You still have to learn this kind of wisdom.
It has to live.
Dwell in this wisdom so that it lives.
Amen.

While I prayed the next day, a risen human became visible. I asked him if I could go over the vision from yesterday, and if I had understood it correctly. Then I became aware of the holy stillness of Christ's grave just before the Easter morning. This was the period when Jesus was in union with God. The risen person spoke:

Yes, Jesus Christ appeared to the women as a figure of light,
to the disciples of Emmaus as a human being,
then passed out of sight again;
afterwards he appeared to the apostles, spoke and ate with them.
He went through walls.
The life of a risen person is to be understood metaphysically.
You don't know this.
The resurrection of Jesus Christ and human beings in general
is metaphysical.
Wisdom is needed to integrate the resurrection
into one's living,
so that one may experience the fullness of life.

I asked if one can do evil after death. The risen human answered:

If someone is in one of the heavens,
then he can do no evil.

There are risen human beings
who have to suffer with compassion for others

because of the wrongdoing that they have caused,
suffer until this wrongdoing has been forgiven and wiped out.

There was the example of a particular old woman
from the Celtic world who had done evil.
Her spirit had to suffer until a stronger person on earth,
together with God, could heal it through prayer.

Crudely put,
she threw mud around and had to stay in it
until someone came and cleaned it up.

In this sense,
evil not yet wiped out
remains as negative energy from those who have died.

Is this difficult to understand?
One day the people will understand it.

21.3.1987
Severino spoke to me:

Do you know what is important in the next world?
The most important thing in eternity is creation.
Everything evolves around creation!
Even healing and helping.
Without love, there is no creation.

After a period of development the focus is on the entire creation.
This period of development is different for each person.

God and Christ are a unity—
they are creation!

Without religion, there is no creation!

Our living in God,
our living with Christ,
gives us light and the Holy Spirit,
and in this way we seek to help;
thus there are thousands of miracles, small and great.

When something becomes whole, healthy, or happy,
this comes from the source—
from God, from Christ.

One has to learn this so as to understand,
regardless of whether one lives in heaven or on earth.

In heaven one lives more intensely,
with more strength and confidence.

*Severino disappeared. The next day I saw him praying and singing
the rosary for someone. He said:*

The rosary gives strength.
It draws strength from all the periods and stages of Jesus' life.

Francis of Assisi added:

Through the rosary you become connected
with Jesus' spiritual force
from his life here on earth.
It is important to know this.

24.3.1987
*Severino spoke about a vision I received several years ago. It was about
Christ, who created a new stage of human development in the period
between Good Friday and Easter morning. From then on, all people
live in eternity on the day they die. Severino continued:*

When you saw and experienced that vision
you arrived at the limits of human existence.
In this period of creation,
from Good Friday to Easter Sunday morning,
a transformation of matter and spirit
into a new level of evolution
took place in and through Jesus Christ.
Only God and Christ can do this.

To contemplate this vision
you need days for your heart to recover.
Give thanks to God for being able to see all these things.

Some days later I saw that Severino radiated light on his right, then on his left side. He said:

Rays of light penetrated me until my risen body radiated light.

1.1.1988
One year later:

The signs of the times are visible:
The sea is rising;
the sky is burning (holes in the ozone layer).
Pray for America, Israel, and Russia.
Pray that the earth does not shudder.

15.1.1988
I died a year ago, and since then I have learned to love.
I have been permitted to love and experience so many things.

Everything is a service to the Lord—to Christ.
I am now capable of loving in a more active way
than when I lived on earth as a human being.

I was born, baptized, and received the Bread of Life.
I now live in the greater life, full of richness!

– 8 –

A Grandmother from Ireland

30.5.1987
A grandmother from Ireland, known to me as Granny, died in 1987.
Before she died, my son Peter spoke as one risen from the dead:

The grandmother from Ireland
believes in the resurrection!
It is a process of development for her.
Give thanks for it!

Severino added:

Granny is about to depart in peace,
trusting in God.
Pray for her often—
for the weaving of light
between heaven and earth.
She will become a person of light.

15.6.1987
*Today the grandmother died. Angels could be seen accompanying her
as a figure of light, as she moved away from the earth. My risen son
Peter spoke to me:*

She is happy as a being of light,
and she sends greetings to you.

Later it was the grandmother herself who spoke:

I see wide fields—wide places—all in light—wonderful!
They are yellow—bright yellow-orange with a bit of red.
A sand-colored path passes through them.

I believe if I go on this path,
new life will begin for me.

16.6.1987
*I saw the grandmother going slowly and carefully on the path she
mentioned yesterday. As she went, she said:*

With every step,
I am changing for the better.

19.6.1987
*I saw the grandmother completing her path of sand. With great care,
she set one foot in front of the other, as if walking on a tightrope.
The last step came, and carefully she stretched out her hand toward an
angel. I saw in vision how she rubbed her forehead gently with her
hand, waited, recovered a bit, and looked again into the distance. She
spoke softly:*

I thank you, O God.
It is all so wonderful and strong.
I thank you, O God.

Then she said to an angel:

Watch over my children
and my grandchildren. Please!

21.6.1987
Today Granny seemed to pass through a door and continued on another path. After two or three steps, she looked below and saw the planet earth. A bright layer of mist parted before her, and she saw the earth, the trees, the houses, and the streets, as if looking through a glass lens. She was very surprised and called out:

I see the earth!

Pensively, yet full of joy, she continued:

I believe the new life is beginning!

22.6.1987
Today I saw the grandmother again. First she looked at Israel; next one by one, at the Mediterranean Sea, the Baltic Sea, the Gulf of Finland, the North Sea, Dublin, and finally the Irish Sea. She then made a small sign of the cross upon herself three times: first on the forehead saying, "In the name of the Father," then on the left shoulder saying, "the Son," then on the right shoulder saying, "and the Holy Spirit." As she said "Amen," her hand was on her breast.

5.7.1987
The grandmother spoke:

I am not suffering,
I am beginning to understand!
I am moving away from the darkness of the earth—
further and further away.

Just before this last vision, Severino spoke about his own path and what the Irish lady was about to experience:

Light streamed through me
until my risen body
had become radiant with light,
could emit light.
This was a purification.
It made me free and happy.
It gives joy!
Granny will experience this development
a week from now.
Let her son rejoice about this!

It is a great thing to experience this level.
I am now free from darkness.
You question me?
Yes! I am free from sin and faulty development
due to my darkness on earth.

Stillness. I could see Severino full of joy and gratitude. He continued:

It is not the same as repentance and the forgiveness of sins;
it is much more a development—a purification,
so that I and others are able to radiate light.
It wasn't just one stage that I had to go through
but many.

19.9.1987
*Today I saw the Irish grandmother looking across a place of brightness.
She was full of joy and said:*

I see Ireland
as it was a long time ago,
in all its beauty and freedom—
when the people laughed and danced
and were strong in their faith.

Silence.

Christ showed me this land
so that I may love it—in prayer before God.

This is my great task,
here in the kingdom of heaven.
I am to live for Ireland—
to help and serve—
so that it again can be free and happy,
rich in spirit and culture,
filled with the faith of the unified church.

4.7.1992
A few years later, the grandmother spoke again:

Quietly the breath of the Holy Spirit will move over Ireland,
and then grow stronger,
to become as a rushing wind.
Pray for this too.
A new period will begin in Ireland.
The light of Jesus Christ is coming,
and it is always preceded by the breath of the Holy Spirit.
This is beautiful, powerful, and holy for me to experience.

– 9 –

A Musician

These next visions are about Franz Eibner, who wrote down most of the hymns I received in vision (see note, p. 173). He was professor of music at the Hochschule für Musik und Darstellende Kunst (Academy for Music and Art) in Vienna. I knew him as "Papa" Eibner.

April 1985
A Risen One said:

Papa Eibner is very ill.
His blood is not enriched with enough oxygen anymore.

I asked: Can we do something for him? The Risen One answered:

No.
Let him be ill in peace,
and be released from the earth.

Low Sunday 1985
*In vision, I saw Franz Eibner. His body was very shaded and dark.
Much light was also with him. Then Christ spoke:*

I come to judge the living and the dead.
Franz Eibner is with the living!

10.3.1986
*Nearly one year later, Franz Eibner died in Perugia, Italy. Four days
later, he was buried at Assisi. Just after his death, he appeared in
vision. He looked straight ahead and said:*

No requiem for the dead!
Resurrection!

Later, a saint spoke:

Mary and angels were with him
in his last days and hours.

To this, Franz said:

Give thanks and sing
"Praise to you, Mary"
and "Glory to Christ, the Lamb of God."
Amen.

*Two days later, I saw Franz turning the leaves of large sheets of music.
I heard him say:*

The key of the C major scale—
this is the foundation point
from which knowledge of music
can emerge.

A minor (A, C, E) is complete.

(*Here I think he meant each chord is a complete world. A minor is a particular world. A minor and C minor relate like partners in a marriage.*)

Listen to the octave! What mysterious wealth!

In the scale, the fundamental is maintained
even if the melody is changed a thousand ways.
These are living vibrations that heal and inform soul and spirit.

The minor key sensitizes.

B minor is a field of rest.
Listen, three or four times,
to the Mass in B minor (Bach),
and you will discover a segment of absolute peace.
It is important for depth psychology
to understand the nature of B minor.

The major key
is like a leaping, skipping stream.
This key should be absorbed into the life of small children,
ten year olds, children prior to puberty,
and those living in the period before marriage—
at these periods of life, it activates and creates joy
that can be absorbed.
The major key is important;
it activates and makes joyful.

When men and women reach a mature age—
from about thirty-five until seventy—
the alternation of minor and major keys
is necessary like physical activity
to activate the spirit and to enliven the body.

The C sharp major scale is not good for heart rhythms.
Prolonged listening can decrease vitality or weaken the heart.

C major, D major, B major, and E flat major stimulate the heart!

19.3.1986
Papa Eibner spoke:

I am a Risen One,
almost a man of light.
I still have to go through
a period of maturity, a time of growing.
This is good.
I rejoice in this development.

20.3.1986
I saw him again. He was studying scores. He looked up and said:

Music is a creation of God.

First there was sound,
beating time,
humming.

Then the passing on of sound melodies—singing.
Words to melodies—sung speech.

Then melody lifted itself out of speech
and expanded,
rhythm and dance were added.
Soul, spirit, and body move in music.

If music is right,
adapted to the development of a people,
then the people evolve!
Then their development is not arrested, does not regress.

Speech, music, and rhythm mold human beings!

Listen!
If this kind of process is rooted in a people—
listen well—
the vessel of the spirit evolves
so that it absorbs religious impulses!
This is a path of increase.

If love, goodness, selflessness, and purity are in a people,
then religion breaks through to them
in all its strength and greatness.
They can make contact with God
and receive light and the Holy Spirit.

To know this is enormous!
Amen.

I saw that Franz was deeply moved by this knowledge. He closed the large book of music and said:

The development of the voice took hundreds of years.

27.3.1986
Franz Eibner spoke to me:

Call the spiritual leaders,
tell them about anthropology—
tell them about creation—
creation in the Old Testament,
creation in the New Testament,
in church history in the first decades.

Tell them of the creation of the human being
and the development of the child until its seventh year
and of the need for love and security when it is really needed.

Tell them about psychology,
and the meaning of dreams, and why people need religion.

Tell them about life after death.

31.3.1986
Franz spoke again:

You will be amazed,
but it is true!
I am alive!
I, Franz Eibner!

The flesh,
that vessel in human form,
this wonderful creation, falls away.
It was like a state of sleep for me when I died.
And then,
with my soul and spirit,
I was truly in a state of radiance, I, the same Franz!
I hear,
I see,
I have speech and thought.
I can praise and glorify.

This state is active in doing and in being.

I see other earths,
other heavenly bodies.
I see human beings and their thoughts.
I see the different peoples
and the whole of creation on earth.

What is new for me are
the people of light.
I have already seen angels.
Paint many angels!

What is new for me is
the "new world"—
the new great region of heaven.
I cannot yet grasp it.
I see and experience it as "patchwork."
I have seen Christ, far away.
I have also seen my parents.
They are not within reach for me.
My little girl who died
I saw as a grown-up figure of light.
She is close to me.

Did I speak to her?
No.

He laughed and said:

I knew that there was an order in heaven.
But here existence has
an unbelievable order—
all according to laws of creation:
God, Christ, the Holy Spirit, angels, the prophets, and saints.

The most loving figure that I saw—
truly an example of love and goodness—
was the mother of Jesus, Mary.
Even though I loved her,
nevertheless it was blindness
that I did not understand her while on earth.

Then, slowly:

Everything is alive here in heaven,
even we Risen Ones,
as part of the greater creation.
You were right in what you wrote:
"In freedom humans live and develop."
Amen.

To participate in the order of creation
is the crowning glory of a risen human being—
serving human beings for Christ.

Created to be human,
our serving in prayer—in heaven as well as on earth—
is the most complete way of living and working.

You do not yet grasp
these laws of existence in the hereafter.
But recognize that we are here, we are present!

All the treasures of the earth are from primal creation.
They are there for you, but they are not yours;
you are only caretakers.

I asked:

Would you prefer to live again on earth?

He answered:

Yes and no.
Yes, in that my family and friends
cannot hear me and cannot speak with me.
No, since everything here is truly more active and complete,
therefore more beautiful.
There is an unfolding of life
without death, illness, or pain as we know it on earth.

I asked: Do you have any further requests? He answered:

Pray for forgiveness,
in that way peace be between all of you and me.
This too is a necessary step, for I often did you wrong.

After some time—some years—
ask and pray that I may help you.

I thank you.

10.4.1986
I saw Papa Eibner surrounded by light, peace, and love. He said:

One step higher, one step further;
three stages are still to be fulfilled.

Sing the hymns you received:
"Praise the Lord" and "Joy, Joy."

18.4.1986
Speak out!
Enlighten people about the angels!
Emphasize the activity of the Holy Spirit!

Once you have written down everything with God's light,
then my task is ended.

Then I asked him about my son Peter. Where was he? He replied:

He is watching us
from the upper region of the kingdom of heaven.

20.5.1986
I saw Franz playing on a grand piano. He struck the keys forcefully with all his fingers. He turned around and said joyfully:

I have understood music!
I will pass on this knowledge to someone on earth
sometime in the future.

He played again on the piano. And then—did I hear it rightly?— he began to sing "Du holde Kunst" by Schubert. Afterward he played an interlude and then, absorbed in the music, he played, as a spring gushing forth, Schubert's "Trout Quintet." It sounded different. An angel spoke:

He is playing it one whole tone higher.

As I sat and prayed, I heard and saw this musician playing music that was sublime.

3.6.1986
I saw Franz again. He said:

Music lives,
immanent in vibrations.
It can be understood scientifically.

It is life,
a creation in the universe, including the earth.
It releases movements of energy.
Its vibrations belong to the creating of the human being.
Humans need music;
it moves soul and spirit—
the nervous system is animated.

Haydn is yet to be explored!

The different rhythms of music
are significant according to each land.

America:
A Haydn would be good for America.
The soul of these people
would become content, joyful, full of love, and balanced.

Europe:
After the sound of drums and the fears of war,
the music of a Grieg, a Chopin, a Ravel, a Liszt
would be wholesome.

Africa:
A Mozart would be good for Africa.

Russia:
A powerful, all-embracing music,
ringing through the forests,
would be right for Russia—
a Beethoven, for instance.

Yes, music is life, movement;
it heals and helps humans unfold.

Then, slowly:

Israel needs the music of its land
over and over again.

6.6.1986
Full of joy, Franz spoke:

My mother lives!

And then, seriously:

Sing three rosaries for my father.
I am grasping, I am comprehending affinities—
the unity of earth, humanity, and God.
A great mystery.

26.10.1989
I saw Franz leaving one level of heaven and moving to another—
into the realm of vibrations. He was about to learn about them. He
looked over this realm a long time and said slowly:

Music . . . the beginning of tones . . . tangible.
I can comprehend it!
O God, O Lord,
give me discernment, then words,
so that I can pass this on.
Amen.

Then, very slowly:

The Primal . . .
Spirit . . .
Light . . .
Life . . .
Yes, life as breath from God.
A movement like breathing . . . high . . . deep . . . in a circle,
quicker, slower.
A whisper . . . the beginning of sound.

He made a sign of the cross on his forehead. Then he stood before an
altar in a church. He held a burning candle in his hand. He knelt
down and prayed.

16.11.1989
Franz spoke again:

The art of the fugue is one step higher
in the laws of music, in the world of sounds.

– 10 –
A Philosopher

M., a professor of philosophy at a well-known Swiss university, died in 1989. He was very disciplined in his approach to philosophy but he was kind and tolerant with his fellow human beings, his colleagues, and his students. It was his students who came and asked me to pray for him. Anyone who knew Professor M. would understand that he is, also in the next world, a person who seeks truth—a person who seeks to comprehend life on earth, in the universe, and in the hereafter. He saw my books. His words spoken about them are to be understood metaphysically. It was two months after his death when I first saw the professor. In a quiet and reflecting way, he spoke to himself:

I am alive!
I understood many things on earth.
I must still comprehend and grow in the life of the spirit.

On earth I was loved.
That was my wealth.
Now I love these people in the presence of Jesus Christ and God.
Greetings to all those who loved me.

Later:

Who will pray a rosary for me daily for five weeks,
as is shown in your book on hymns?
I will hear them and give thanks.

An angel said:

He will be at the Wailing Wall in Jerusalem for three weeks,
and afterwards on the hill of Golgotha for five weeks.

Some time later, I saw that the professor was looking over my work So That You May Be One (*in German,* Ein Fels I *and* II). *The German volumes lay open, an arch of light above them. The professor read from them and, deep in thought, quoted Genesis 3:12–24: "Accursed be you of all animals wild and tame..." He spoke:*

This is not the truth.
It is mythical.
God does not punish or curse the soil,
or an animal, or a human being.
God did not curse Eve.

Then he spoke to his loved ones and friends on earth:

I am now going to travel through
A period of early history—
through the Old Testament and later through the New Testament.
In order to integrate the history of humankind
within myself
I will—I may—travel over lands and seas.
I will live in the fullness of being.

Weeks later, the professor became visible. He spoke with a saint and asked him a question which had occupied his students and caused a lot of discussion:

Is there reincarnation?

This was a question that had occupied him with his students. The saint replied:

No. But there is a great evolution of creation and of humankind
—that has been given.

The saint said to me:

You know about the informative pattens given to humans
and about their development through God's Spirit.
Don't turn aside!

The professor said:

I want to assimilate this process of evolution
within myself
insofar as God permits.

I bow down before God.
Silence.

*After these words, I asked Professor M. about his experiences after
death, and he answered:*

I awoke,
as if after a light sleep,
and then calmly contemplated
my body of light.

My head was shining—
filled with a thousand points of light.
There was a center of concentrated light
in one part of my head.

The form of head and body
was the same as on earth,
except it was made out of light
and animated with spirit.

The whole body—of light and spirit—was present in this way.
There was movement, listening, speech.
But there was no hunger.

A vessel full of movement and strength
was present at the level of the breast:
This was my soul.

A new life—
a life of joy and full of expectation.

Then I saw that great errors were made on earth!
Errors in the use of chemistry,
not only on the earth, but also in its surroundings.
Errors in medicine.
Great errors committed through lack of love and lack of the
          spirit.
Errors from the misuse of power.

I recognized many things on the earth.
I have still to grow in the realm of the spirit.

In the following visions I saw him contemplating the beginnings of life on earth. I saw him in a place with much water: a sea on the left side and desert on the right. In this desert was a green area with plants that were clearly recognizable. He observed a transformation here— how the cell and its nucleus changed, and how the area became green. He observed the changes in the plants by means of the light. This phase of creation held him spellbound.

A few days later I saw him observing a stalk extending itself upwards out of a small green plant, and seeing how a blossom came into being from its green leaves. The leaves were narrower and longer than those of a tulip. Within the blossom was a small yellow pistil. The diameter of the stalk was hexagonal, hairy, and slightly thorny. The roots of these plants were short. The professor was astonished and said slowly:

The first flower
out of which the entire variety of blossoms developed.
A miracle—that I have been permitted to see.

A tear rolled down his cheek.

A few days later, I saw him looking over the green area and the water. Thirty centimeters above them was a blue layer, perhaps of light or gas. This layer slowly emitted rays to the green plants—right into their roots—and into the water. Far in the background, the same thing happened from a red layer. He spoke:

Years later came yellow.
I have witnessed three miracles:
the transformation of the cell in plants,
through which they later became green;
the first flower;
color—how it came to be in the process of creation.
Water, desert, earth, plants, flowers, trees, blossoms, and fruits:
All these I witnessed as part of the processes of growth.

The first animals that I was permitted to see were
giant whalelike creatures in the water,
and then crawling animals
coming out of the water onto the land.

Some weeks later, he continued:

A new epoch began at that stage of creation
when a being was created
whose spirit was and is above all other beings:
the human being!
A great stage in evolution!
You cannot understand this!

*Then I was shown an open hut of leaves, supported by the trunks
of trees. A small group of light brown people—men, women, and
children—was in the hut. The professor saw such groups in different
places. An angel spoke about this:*

Five hundred years passed
since the coming into being of the first human.

He added, reflecting:

The beginning of human history.

*Some days later I saw in vision the professor observing human beings
after five thousand years of further development. He spoke:*

To see the spiritual evolution of humanity
is new for me!

And then, in a state of contemplation, he added:

There is God, light, and the Holy Spirit.
There are the angels, who are human in form.
There are those who are risen from the dead.
One can see a spiritual link from those in heaven
to the people on earth.

An angel said:

These links enable humans to evolve further.

The professor said:

Points of light—as informative patterns—
entered mainly the cerebrum,
all this happening within the order of creation.

The Jewish people have found their place
within this order.
They experienced and lived
this kind of relationship with God,
even though it happened thousands of years later.

Since the creation of man and woman,
there were always chosen people
who were strong in spirit
and who experienced the link with God!

Then, slowly:

The wholeness of soul, spirit, and body—
entire races cultivated this reality.
A natural, instinctive love,
the source of security and protection was present.
These were people who were truly human
and secure in God.

Some days later, the professor spoke again:

My experiences, development, and understanding
continue in Jerusalem.
There I will remain at the Wailing Wall
and its surroundings
for three weeks.
I rejoice that in spirit
I am allowed to see
the period of the Old Testament.
I see that in front of the Wailing Wall
there is an invisible layer,
about one meter in width, containing information
about the people and the land.
The density of its spirit is strong and overpowering.

Some time later, he added:

The attacks against the people of ancient Israel
were as if hounds got a whiff of a stronger spiritual presence!

Three days later he said:

The life of the figures of the Bible impresses me greatly.
They are joyful, strong people.
We could use such people today!
Death was not their enemy,
it was only a small interruption
on the path to eternal life with the ancestors.
This impressed me greatly.
Love these people!

Four days later he was happy to see some of the figures of the Old Testament. He called out:

Abraham! Isaac! Rebecca! Rachel! David!

Moses was out of reach, but the professor saw him far away and recognized him. Later he said:

The wars in the Old Testament are a horror for me,
but the laws formed the people of Israel.
They gave them an ethic.
Later the prophets were of great significance!
Through the prophets
light descended on the people
and on wide areas of land.
I rejoice!

Then I saw and heard how a saint gave thanks and praise for the lives of the prophets, singing the hymn I received in vision:

Jubilation and singing,
sounding and trembling,
upward to Thee,
O God.
Spirit moving,
Spirit quickening,
Spirit breathing and hovering.
Joy! Rejoicing!
Jubilation resounds!

Some days later, the professor spoke again:

A field of light—gentle and pure—
came to earth with Isaiah.
It was an anticipation of Christ's birth.

Then, to me:

Do you see it?
So many years in advance, light was given
for the great turning point—for the era of light and Spirit.
One should live through the Old Testament in a new way
so as to grasp, understand, and live in the new era.
Acknowledge this!

I have grown to love the Wailing Wall
with its strong message of the Spirit,
and I rejoice that I may experience the period of Christ's birth.

He continued:

I will remain here for several days
and take within myself the beautiful warm light.

The holy period is approaching within reach of my experience.

I saw Mary.
She had light around her head—
points of light shone like blossoms of flowers.

Later Joseph and Mary saddled a donkey
and went from Nazareth to the river Jordan.

After some days, the professor continued with his account:

Nazareth, Bethlehem, Golgotha:
the points of encounter between light and earth.
Love them!

On the level of spirit and image,
I absorbed within myself Nazareth.
This I did with my eyes, my breath, and my soul.
I dwelt there for three days.

The path that Mary and Joseph took to Bethlehem
was long, very long.
The first third of the way was full of light and joy.
The second third was difficult, but God's strength could be felt.
The last part of the journey was completed bit by bit.

Now Joseph spoke:

For Mary's sake, we rested often by the Jordan.
She was very loving and full of peace.
She was often motionless before God, her lips moving.
From time to time she sat noble as a queen, on the donkey.
As a queen she rode into the town of Bethlehem.

The shepherds experienced the holy night
as you described it in your book of hymns.

The professor then described the three wise men:

One wise man came out of Upper Egypt,
another came from the Nile area,
and the third came from the north of Lebanon.

I also saw that when Mary left their lodgings,
a young woman, dressed in blue, looked after the child Jesus.

The flight of Joseph, Mary and the child
ended in Egypt, not far from the frontier.
From there they traveled along the Jordan back to Nazareth.

The spirit of Jesus could be discerned in public
when he was twelve years of age
among the teachers in the temple.
Powerful rays of light went forth from him, wherever he was.

Professor M. turned the pages of the first volume of So That You
May Be One *and spoke:*

You described Mark's gospel very well.
It is good that you recorded everything in this way.

He smiled:

Matthew, too, was the way you described him.
Perhaps you will receive more information later.
Luke—yes, Luke the wise one,
who discerned, researched, and wrote down everything.
He was often with Mary, the mother of Jesus.
You could complete your account
with other visions you have received—
especially about the sufferings, death, and resurrection of Jesus.
You described well Peter's greatness, and Paul's—
that warrior of the spirit.
To understand John is grace, is light, is life.
For myself, I call this fire of compassion.
It is here that I begin with the faith.
I pray and ask for the inspiration of the Holy Spirit,
so that Christians in the church may discern
the Johannine church in your visions.
Peter died the death of a martyr, Paul likewise.
John lived in Ephesus.
He lived as a man of light.
He built a church.
He built a house for Mary on the hill (overlooking Ephesus).
Love this site.
Mary was buried in Ephesus, in the church garden.
Dig out the scrolls on the straight street of Ephesus.
This is very important.

He spoke slowly:

Christianity... Philosophy...
Christianity and the philosophical thinking
of the early Celtic church from the British Isles
were spiritual influences present in Europe
for over three hundred years.
Their influence was mostly positive.
Traces are still to be found today.
But the philosophers have not recognized John up to now.

They have not realized the great turning point
that came with Christ.
This is a weakness—a mistake—in philosophical thinking.
We too carry responsibility for the spiritual chaos.
Temptation, the striving for power,
weighs the scale down a lot: Sin!

I will now go before God and worship!
To be truly human
is to live in God with Christ,
and to be linked with the Holy Spirit!
Let the peoples of the earth develop and grow!
Let every person live his or her life in freedom.
Let all humans live with love for each other.
May each one carry the other's burden.

Some weeks later he said:

You experienced with me how I saw the pregnancy of Mary
and the long path through the valley of the Jordan to Bethlehem.
I saw the shepherds and the women with Mary.
I saw the three wise men, who had come a long way.
Nazareth and Bethlehem
were powerful experiences for me.
I did not see Mark at the manger.
He was to be seen in a house.
He was deep in thought and praying before God
as the news from Bethlehem arrived.
What I later saw were the workings of Jesus as a grown man—
how light, spirit, life came to many people.
To observe all this was new to my spirit,
new to my sensitivity and understanding.
For days and weeks,
I saw the workings of the Spirit and light flowing from Jesus.
John grasped the fullness of the Spirit, of light, and of creation
through Christ as he worked among the people.
They were transformed!

Some days later, the professor went from this part of heaven, where he saw and understood so much, to another, brighter place of light. He said to himself:

Christ brought all that to humankind,
gave it to them for their development.
It is more than humans have recognized.
Some mystics and artists have given a hint of it—
a Michelangelo, a Mozart, a Bernadette.
Human beings are complete
when they live according to Christ's teachings for his disciples,
when they take in light and open themselves to the Holy Spirit.
This is the right way to live.
To recognize this,
you need praying people
who ask for the link to God.
You need teachers of the faith
who explain the New Testament in a real way.
You need trained philosophers
who study the thoughts and ways of the people.
You need psychologists
who help people find the way to God.
Only in this way will love and peace
be among individuals and the peoples of the earth.
Praying, I step forward before Christ.
May he receive me in his service, as small as I am.
I want to help individuals and the peoples of the world
to live in an authentic way.

Then he said:

To walk for a whole day in the light
is the most beautiful way of being on earth!

After some days, he spoke again:

I am returning to Jerusalem.

It is true that Mary fled by the sea route from Israel to Ephesus.

He continued in a state of contemplation:

Patrick, the patron saint of Ireland, was a figure of light.
Light came from heaven to earth—
there where light already was.

The rays of light from the stars
shine very intensely in Nazareth.

Some time later he added:

Part of the history of humankind,
and the search for a common bonding among humans,
is recorded in the story of Israel.
This story represents a large part
of the development of the human spirit.
"Israel" also signifies that period of development
which came through Jesus.
He brought light and he brought life after death
to every human being.
He made possible for us the link with the Holy Spirit.
He is the Christ who gives life.

A new period began then;
that is why I returned to Jerusalem.

In Nazareth the angel announced to Mary
the birth of the child Jesus.
Light came to Bethlehem through this birth.
There was also intense light in Jerusalem at the crucifixion
of Jesus.

I wish to linger in these three places—
Nazareth, Bethlehem, and Jerusalem—
to strengthen my being, my spirit, my soul.
Amen.

Write everything down!

*Later in vision I saw the professor in the village of Nazareth. I could
see a great field of light. The rays were ordered in geometric forms and*

were spread out over large areas of the earth. Then the professor spoke slowly:

This is life—rays of life.
These rays reach every Christian on earth.
Rejoice over this!
These rays go through my body like pinpricks.

I asked if they could heal the sick and he answered:

I can't answer that.
In order to do so, something has to happen to my spirit.
What is new for me is this experience of light.
These rays of light reach Christians
and give them the light of life—imperishable light.
By living the Christian way of life,
light spreads to everyone.

I asked once more if one should go from time to time to Nazareth and stay there for a while. He answered:

To stand in Nazareth on top of the hill in the open air,
praying with arms apart,
works miracles and brings great joy to the soul.
Open your soul and spirit to God.
I will remain here, so that I may understand it all.
Here the angel spoke to Mary.
Mary answered, and then it happened:
Life, light (*in many colors*) and the Holy Spirit
descended to Mary—came into her—and brought Jesus to life.

He continued:

Life, light, and Spirit moved Mary—and the whole earth.
This happened in Nazareth.

Some days later:

Now that I have experienced creation,
through the workings of the Holy Spirit,

a gate is opening out toward a distant horizon,
toward the universe.
A new area of creation for me!

I asked if that means a new opening for culture, music, and religion.
He continued:

I shall return, in spirit.
My path here in the afterlife is the right path for me personally,
so that I become whole!
Time on earth—that is right for the soul.

I serve where God will have me.
I give thanks that I may pass all this on to you.
Amen.

Later he said:

To serve God is a royal task.
Now I can serve—
serve those who are mentally ill on earth,
serve those whose spirit has been deformed by others.

Suns, moons, mists, and gases of the heavens—
who can understand the greatness of God?

Some months later, the professor spoke once more:

What is a human being?
A creation of God:
a being who is capable of developing the spirit,
a being who can be linked with the Creator,
a being who can receive light from God's light.
This is light that remains in the human being
until he or she develops to become a person of light.
God created the human as the crown of creation.
God created a being, who lives on after life on earth is over,
if light is within him or her.
Risen human beings live an extensive, inclusive,
powerful, all-embracing life.

– 11 –
A Pianist

W., a pianist, was a friend of our family. After he died, I saw him for the first time in a vision on February 13, 1985. As one risen from the dead, he continued a conversation that we once had while he was on earth:

You are right.
The four greatest musicians who lived on earth were
Mozart, Schubert, Liszt, and Grieg.
Others, like Bach, Handel, and Beethoven were great musicians, but the first four were the most important.

1.3.1985
The pianist spoke again:

Practice singing!
It creates vibrations in the body,
as does music (*with instruments*).
When listening to music:
move with it, go with the rhythm, enter the experience!
Even if you are just listening to it!

– 12 –
A Sculptor

These are visions about a well-known sculptor. He was a larger than life figure who lived to the full. He was not at all religious, nor did he raise his family to be religious. He died from a heart attack in 1989. I could see him in the next world, in an area that was light gray. On the day of his death, he spoke to himself:

Angels are with me.
They are protecting me and showing me the way—
the path of development toward the greater life.
I am at peace; I trust completely and rejoice that heaven is open.
There are new dimensions to life!

Then he asked:

Will you (*friends and people whom he knew*)
pray eight rosaries for me—the rosaries of the resurrection?

Later:

I love; I am loved by my family and friends.

That evening he exclaimed with joy:

I see light!
I see figures of light!

2.4.1989
He cried out in astonishment:

I am alive!
I . . . I . . . am alive!
Great God.

And that evening:

A new world!
I am beginning to grasp, to sense
and want to understand everything.
New dimensions!
A new dimension of spirit.
God . . . is God.
Jesus Christ is his son.
The angels live.
They sing, they speak, they help humankind.
Mary, I did not know you.
I regret it.
I want to love you.
I marvel that there is a Holy Spirit that comes from God.

The Holy Spirit is active and passes on messages.
The Holy Spirit is available to human beings.

Little by little I am moving through this new world.
I want to be active, to help people on earth,
I want to do so on a large scale!

Adding slowly:

If that is possible.

I asked: Are you happy that you are lying in the graveyard, under a stone that you yourself made? He answered:

At the moment this is absolutely unimportant to me.

4.4.1989
In my vision, I heard him saying:

Christ descended into hell.
The other risen people and I were not in hell,
We were not in what you call the underworld,
the realm of the dead.

Then he asked himself: What is hell? What is the underworld? Silence followed. An angel, carrying a small book, approached. The angel stood before the sculptor and said:

Listen!
In the story of humankind,
a long development was necessary after physical death,
so that humans could work and be active from the afterlife.
With the religion in the period of the Old Testament,
a further unfolding of human beings took place on earth
and their presence in the underworld was shortened.
Through the life of Jesus Christ among you
and through his death,
the powers of the underworld were overcome entirely.
From then on, humans could evolve on earth
in a more intensive way.
New life ... yes, life ... entered human beings.

Then the angel asked the sculptor:

Have you understood?

The sculptor answered slowly:

Yes.
Easter is a great feast in the Eastern Orthodox Church.

And, in a state of contemplation, he described five steps in a heavenly ladder:

Leaving the body,
an opening to existence, "becoming,"
purification,
further development of soul and spirit,
a new ability to work for God.

I am on a path of becoming.
I rejoice over the period of purification.
Where I was hard with others,
I hope to serve and help with love
until the damage and hardness I inflicted
have been healed.
From the outset I wish to let religion,
to let God and Jesus Christ,
penetrate my spirit once again.
In this way I will be joined with Christ.
In this wholeness I will work with Christ in the greater life.

And looking to the earth:

Is there anyone on earth
who will pray for me and love me
as I go on the path of becoming?
I see one ... two ... five people who love me.
I see them as points of light on the earth.

Silence followed, and I saw the angel move away. The next day I prayed, and he spoke to me again:

Peace has come to me through discernment. Amen.

8.4.1989
The sculptor:

A further step is to recognize movement
in the basic patterns of life.
It is to be found in the rhythms of classical music,
in the beating of the drums of Africa,
in the movement of the leaf
or the ceremonial rods of the North American Indians.
The rhythm of language is different.

11.4.1989
The sculptor showed me a table with drawings on it. He said:

Art begins in small things.
First the basic forms must be present...
The composition of greater works comes later,

Adding slowly:

a line, a square, a triangle, a cube,
and a circle as a symbol of completion.

Then speaking seriously:

Listen!
The faith of a people shows itself in their art.
What about today?
Inspire with encouragement, testimonies, forms, and colors!
Think about this!
All of you, think about this!

Later:

A red point grew to a red star;
then its spirit lost its color and died out—
all this through the calling of prayer!

(*I understood him to be speaking about the rise and fall of Communism.*)

12.4.1989
The sculptor:

I have come into the realm of the angels and Mary.
Here I see women of strength and power.

He stood before them, then bowed before them and begged for forgiveness:

Forgive me,
I was presumptuous toward women.
Truly I respect you, but I was presumptuous!

There was stillness. Then he said:

Receive my thanks
for having been able to see the greatness of risen women.
Men and women are people of light.
Nothing separates us.
We are figures of light—risen humans.
Forgive me.

Then he looked at Mary:

Mary...?
The realm of angels
is a new experience for me.
Give me time to absorb all of this.

I want to return to earth again
so that I may sculpt real angels!

And then he said to me:

Paint! Paint!
Paint as long as strength is given to you!
Please! It is so important.

He looked back at the angels a long time and then said to himself:

I am nothing... dust.

13.4.1989

The sculptor moved on a path of light. Afterwards he looked out over a huge area, as big as Europe. It symbolized the future development of science, physics, and to some extent chemistry on earth. He surveyed everything, trembled, and said:

It frightens me!

Then he asked if he could go on to the planets. I saw him move through an area resembling a forest in color and density. When he came out of it, he could look toward the stars. He could see the formation of a planet at close range. The substance around the planet was uneven, whitish in color, and contained particles of dust and sand. Water dripped and flowed out of it. Some dark patches were also visible. He then asked an angel: How long does this formation take? The angel answered:

Millions of years (*until it becomes a solid mass*).

The sculptor said:

Can I have some of this water to study?

The angel replied:

No. It is poisonous; it contains uranium.

The sculptor asked:

And the white, damp mass? Can I have some of that to study?

The angel said:

No. It is important to know that if it was brought to the earth
        now
it would cause damage.
You have seen a few hours in creation.
Be grateful for that.

The sculptor retreated meditating, with his head bowed. Later I could see him reflecting about everything, and slowly he said:

I have experienced so many things:
a flash of heaven, earth, and creation.

I want to go before God.
If it so pleases, I want to ask God this:
Give me the possibility to go back to earth
with these new revelations so as to build anew.
This is so urgent.
Or please show me how I can serve you,
the earth, and creation from here.
I implore you.

Later he spoke to me:

Then I saw Christ.
He looked at me seriously and said:
We were good to you
because you are a person who seeks the truth,
and we have shown you realms of heaven.
Purify yourself; grow in the life of the spirit.
Learn to understand the Father, the Son, and the Holy Spirit.
When this strength is in you, work for the earth.
Amen.

Some days later, Christ spoke to me:

He saw the formation of a planet.
His words and experiences are important steps
in the right sequence.

24.4.1989
The sculptor spoke:

I have seen Moses!
What a gift!

And some days later, once again:

There must be guidance
so that humans become human in the image and likeness of God.
There must be justice, truth, and freedom of the spirit.
Observing humans and understanding them
purely from a psychological perspective is not enough.

The task of the psychologist
is to lead them into greater dimensions of life.

Love of your neighbor and serving the poorest
is the highest level of being.
You will fulfill the law of love in this way.
Amen.

I bow down before God.

– 13 –
A Writer

This writer was an elderly woman, a graphic artist, and author of a book. She died in 1992. A few days after her death, an angel appeared to me and spoke:

She is alive!
She lives in great joy and implores you to continue to write.

Then the writer appeared and said:

Now I see the angels!
Give my greetings to L. (*a mutual friend*).
She has to take care of her health and eat fresh fruit.

The next day, she spoke again:

I have not understood all of Christianity,
and could not take it all within me.
You are to write everything down that has been given to you.
Please do!
You have received Christianity in its fullness.

That evening:

The world cries out for help!

Two days later:

I am now experiencing the history of the people of Israel.
Pray for Israel!
Life in the next world is far-reaching, powerful,
and cannot be understood.
I am astounded.
I walk step by step as a risen being of light,
and I give thanks that I was prepared for this on earth,
living with the Jewish and Christian heritage.

Then she said to me:

I ask you to pray for me from time to time.
You will see the stages that I go through here, in life after death.
One of the stages is to understand the concentration camps.

Four months later I saw this writer in contact with many people, especially children suffering from famine in Africa. She was very earnest as she brought help to those people.

– 14 –
A Psychologist

A., a psychologist, died from a stroke in 1991. A friend of hers asked me to pray for her. In vision, I saw a saint who asked that we pray again and again the glorious mysteries of the rosary. Several days later, this saint made the sign of the cross three times, saying:

In the name of the Father, the Son, and the Holy Spirit.

As the saint made the sign of the cross, a red light appeared, which meant suffering. An angel spoke about this:

Ask your close friends to pray that the link to the Son,
the link to primal light, may come into being.

Nearly two weeks later, the psychologist spoke as one risen from the dead. She was in a deep state of reflection:

I thank you for your prayers.
I have experienced so much in my life.
While on earth, I took in and understood many things.
Yet I did not accept Jesus as Christ, as the Messiah.

I see a path of light and I will go on it—toward Christ.
Pray for me now, in these days.
Give thanks!

– 15 –
Friedrich Nietzsche

23.10.1990
Today I received a visit from a professor of history. This lady had been staying near Sils Maria in the upper Engadin, where Nietzsche spent the last few years of his life. During a long discussion, she explained to me Nietzsche's philosophy and emphasized his search for the truly human. That evening after she had left, I put these questions aside and wanted to forget the whole conversation. However, the next day while I was in prayer, Nietzsche appeared to me. He stretched out his hand to me and said:

I ask you . . .
Go before God for me,
and pray that all the stages
which you have now seen
can continue to develop in my soul,
but even more in my spirit, in my spiritual life.

I ask you further
to overcome with prayer
all the negative consequences

that have come into being,
through the presence of my spirit,
when I lived on earth among the people.

Except for a few,
they have not been able to grasp or understand
my searching, my soul, my spirit.
I am beginning... to become aware...
You must remain clear and firm in your spiritual life.
Don't be misled!

– 16 –
Galileo Galilei

1.5.1990
*As I prayed, suddenly Galileo stood in front of me. I saw his pronounced
features and a critical, inquiring look in his eyes. He spoke:*

I am Galileo Galilei.
There is a big mistake in the measurement
of the space-time continuum, in the space telescope.

*He looked as if he was examining something, and then I saw him no
more. I could not say a word. I was so perplexed. Did he speak so that I
could realize that he is still alive today? Does he too work as one risen
from the dead? I spoke about this vision with some friends and even
made some witty remarks, thinking it was very odd that Galileo, who
lived in the sixteenth century, would talk to me. One month after the
vision, the newspapers reported that a great mistake had been made
in cutting the reflector of the Hubble telescope.*

– 17 –
The Risen People of Japan

May 1993

On the day I returned from my holidays, I learned that Mrs. G., a gentle, loving lady whom I knew from our village, had suddenly died. She died in old age, having lived a very active life and helping many in our community. She had traveled in the East with her husband and his students, and had lived in Japan for ten years. That evening I prayed for my friend who loved the Orient, especially Japan, simply asking God for grace, light, and a healing of all the shadows that had accumulated in the course of her life. I then saw my friend in the hereafter. She was in a room filled with a bright gray light. With her were several Japanese people, risen from the dead. As she entered the room, she had to stoop because the ceiling was low. I was sure this kind of room had a symbolic significance. My friend began to speak with the Japanese people:

I have come to greet you!

I could see that these risen Japanese responded joyfully.
She continued to talk to the risen Japanese:

I will now talk to you about the life of the spirit after death among the different peoples of the world.

The Christians and the people of Israel believe in one God,
who created heaven and earth.
They believe that God created
a link between heaven and earth through Christ.
They believe in a power that is active and effective
between God and humankind—the Holy Spirit.
All this enables a continuous development of the human spirit.

There are peoples of the world,
such as the people of India, China, Japan,
and other peoples in the East,

who have their spiritual roots on earth.
Their ancestors are their help after death.

My friend spoke joyfully:

I never knew that there is a further development after death
for the peoples of the East
in which their ancestors accompany them.

They will evolve step by step
until they enter a radiant bright blue place
that looks like a high plateau of rock.

Later they will go on a path without their ancestors
into an area of pure light.
There all people are linked with God and serve him.

My friend then said with kindness:

This is not a path of suffering,
nor is it a path to be dreaded.
It is one on which these people evolve to become people of light.

I asked about the path after death for the people of Africa or Australia.
My friend answered:

I only see, far away in the distance,
that there is a similar development of life after death
for other peoples, especially for the people of Africa.

I am happy that I could experience this,
because I love Japan.
Japan is in my heart.

Write all this down.
I don't know if I will meet or speak to you again.

Shortly afterwards, a young man wanted to know more about the risen
people of the East. I prayed about his questions, and an angel replied:

These ancestors are risen human beings, risen in eternal life.
They are not yet linked with Christ.

*It was during this period that Christ appeared to me and spoke about
a passage in the Bible (Luke 9:59–60):*

"Leave the dead to bury their dead" means:
Do not shed tears when someone dies.
Live with the risen people in a Christian way!
For I, Christ, have risen from the dead,
and your fellow human beings have risen from the dead too!
They are alive!

January 1995
*Nearly two years later, friends of mine felt that not enough had been
said about the religions of the people of the East, especially about their
having spiritual roots on earth, and wanted to know if this applied to
Buddhism. After I had sat a long time in the church, a very ancient
holy man stood before me. He was dressed in a cowl that looked like a
covering of moss. He had lived on earth in the Nile Valley a long time
ago, probably before the time of Moses. He spoke:*

Listen!
Buddhism is meditation, beholding oneself from within,
so as to grasp the ineffable in humans, animals, plants—
the entire world.
It is not a seeking
but an embracing of everything within oneself
to enable soul and spirit to evolve,
and to find the essential truth of life as well.
That is the religion—the meditation—of the Oriental peoples.
It is an expression of deep roots reaching back to primal man!
Acknowledge this!
It expresses the first step
in the spiritual development of humankind.
Years, millions of years, were needed until the human evolved
to the point of being able to encounter God.
The first ones to experience this were individuals
like Abraham, Isaac, Moses,
and others, as recorded in the Old Testament.

Again thousands of years were needed before soul and spirit
had developed enough to receive Jesus Christ
as the one who gives light, life, and the Holy Spirit.
This was so that humans could work and be active
for other humans and for the earth,
in this life and later when risen from the dead.

Then the holy man from the Nile spoke again:

Move through the primal period of human life on earth slowly,
stage after stage.
Reflect about the period from Moses to the period of Christ.
Reflect on the time between Christ's death, his resurrection,
and then Pentecost.
Then reflect on the period of the Christian people,
the theologians, and the church.
A new period is coming into being.
It is the Johannine period.

All of you, Buddhists and Christians,
hold out your hands to one another.
Behold the great line in the evolution of humankind.

– 18 –
My Husband

December 1991
*During the entire month, I saw in vision angels and many figures of
light around the bed of my husband. I knew then that he would not
live much longer. He died on the 29th of December. After a while, I
saw him going on a path ascending toward the heavens. He spoke:*

I am going to Christ.
I am on the way toward him.

He looked upon the earth, saw many points of light, and said to me slowly:

As Christians we lived in the movement of creation.

On the day of his burial, I heard him say:

I love you all.
I thank you for your love.
Remain together.

10.1.1992
Today I saw him with his mother. She was full of peace. Afterwards he saw his father, who contained much life and light within himself, in another realm of heaven. He spoke to his father:

The earth is in a process of evolution for all human beings.
You, father, are more active—more in this process—
because music is within you.
(*As a musician on earth, he absorbed music within himself.*)
I am on the way to Christ,
full of hope, full of joy.

Our son Peter, risen from the dead, added:

He is not alone on this path to Christ,
and yet he experiences it for himself personally—as an individual!
There are thousands of figures of light around him—
many Christians.
They are all in the process of becoming risen humans.
They also experience the fields of light.

Peter turned to me and said:

I rejoice when you too can be here,
and we can experience this together!

Later, on the same day, I saw Peter showing his father a corona far away in the universe, from which many yellow rays of light beamed forth. My husband asked:

What is that?

Peter said:

A new world is being created.
The arch is filled with rays of light.
It is the beginning of an earth.
Your task is to experience the coming into being of a new earth.
This is the spirit of creation.
Then you will understand many things on earth—
also why Christians must find unity.

*Some weeks later my husband could behold some stages of the earth's
evolution. He spoke about them:*

The first clouds could be seen as vapors.
Then came "green" and "blue" over the earth—
first water, plants, small trees,
later dinosaurs emerged from the waters—
all this over a period of billions of years.
Then I saw small animals, like rats,
and larger animals, like the horses of today.
Light appeared: the first human being.
And man and woman looked toward the sun and the stars.
I could hear the beatings of the winds, storms, and rain!
I saw the first community of human beings.
I heard the mumbling, whistling, and voicing of different sounds!
I saw their first laughter and first tears,
their bursts of rage when in danger, their fights with animals.
They ran and they climbed.
Over a period of five million years,
human life established itself on earth—
life from God's creation!

After humans had already inhabited the earth for a million years,
light penetrated the left half and later the right half of the brain.
(*Light spread over the forehead, nose, and eyes.*)
Through this development of the cerebrum,
the human spirit began to evolve—
a process that brought into being
the link between God and humans!

Angels, messengers from heaven,
and the breath of the Holy Spirit
were manifest on earth.
Much joy was present at this stage of spiritual development!

In the second million years of human existence,
humans evolved very quickly.
They overcame great distances,
worked, and defended themselves with stones and sticks.
When they moved across the land, children went with them.
In the second half of this period, they began to hunt.
(*Before this they lived as vegetarians.*)
They struck out at fishes and other animals.
From then on, they wore animal skins.
Behold: there were clans.
There was no fighting among the clans;
instead they were ready to help one another!
The women were together with the children,
the men with each other and with the older boys.

He cried out with joy:

Look there! Can you see that?
Then began the meeting of their spirits,
when they attempted to understand each other.
Peace was with them.
Write down:
They were not conscious of good and evil.
There was no Cain and Abel.
That was the beginning of a great period,
in which the human spirit evolved!

He gazed over the earth once again and said:

Behold the human being, created by God.
The first transparent spiritual link
between God and humankind became visible.
Humans have evolved since then and will continue to evolve.

Pray to God that men and women, linked with God,
base their further development on the spirit of creation.
Amen.

Peter said to him:

God's Spirit has been active among humans
over hundreds of thousands of years.
Look at those points of light—
signs of the development of the cerebrum and cerebellum.
These are the processes of growth for all human beings:
God's creation over thousands, over millions, of years!

Now you see your life and your wife's life
as points of light, as lifelines on earth.
You lived loving God, Christ, and the Holy Spirit,
loving your fellow humans and all creatures,
who attempted to live in God's creation.
As Christians, you sought to live in the wholeness of creation.
To live in the wholeness of creation
is to live on earth and in the next world.

Some months later I asked my husband to support a group of people.
He answered:

The purpose of my being right now is to be with a sick person.
If Christ asks me, I will be with this group of people.
I am often among theologians and in the churches!
It is important and good for them that I am risen from the dead!
Yes—God's plan is magnificent!

For many years now, I have participated in prayer at the Lord's Sup-
per and taken the Eucharist every day. I received it in vision from
Protestant, Catholic, or Orthodox priests. Today, just after Easter, I
saw my husband in vision in our Reformed church. He approached me
with strength and peace and handed to me the bread and chalice. I
was overjoyed that he could serve in the church in this way.

On the Sunday after Easter, I saw him in the presence of risen
theologians. He was with Cyril of Beloozero, Nicholas von Flue, Bir-
gitta of Sweden, Francis of Assisi, Conall of Ireland, and Quakers

from England. A few times he was with Mary Magdalene, who fights for God's ways. I dared to ask him what he was doing with these theologians. He answered:

We ask Christ that we may help, serve, and be active
in the spiritual development of Christians and the churches.
We see and hear what is happening
among Christians and the churches.

Some time later a saint said:

Call for the help of the risen theologians and people of learning,
that they may show the politicians the true and authentic way
to resolve the plight of the refugees from Yugoslavia.

– 19 –

cA Friend in Heaven

An artist, known to me, had just lost his male partner. He was deeply upset and had great difficulty overcoming this loss. I prayed, and an angel answered:

Although he did not live the fullness of creation—
the wholeness of man and woman—
he lived as a kind-hearted and noble human being.
As a man on earth, his link to God was of light.
It was strong and pure.
He is loved, and he is in the light of God.
He asks you to pass on this message:
"Live with joy.
Be kind and full of love for your fellow humans.
Do this in the lesser life on earth,
and rejoice for the greater life in heaven!"

Adding joyfully:

"Life in the next world is in many ways greater,
more beautiful, magnificent, and full of light!
Do not be afraid!"

– 20 –
An Unborn Child

*I knew a young woman who loved children and wished she had one of
her own. In fact she had been pregnant three times but each time lost
her child before it was born. I talked with her often, and once I asked
her if the child whom she had lost in the third month of pregnancy
would now be about eight years old. She nodded in affirmation and
I told her that I had seen in a vision an angel speaking of her child.
The angel said:*

The child lives and will grow up to be a person of light.
May she (*the mother*) rejoice!

*Later I saw the child, about eight years old, in the hereafter. She looked
at her mother and spoke:*

When something beautiful and great happens to you,
then share it with me.

Then the girl turned to me and said:

Mami never made a picture book for me.
When she plays the piano,
then she should play once especially for us
(*a sign that all three children are alive*).

*From then on, this young mother suddenly discovered a new rela-
tionship to her three children, whom she had thought were dead. For
months she worked on this relationship until a deep and loving contact*

became established. She herself felt more balanced, aware that her soul and spirit had been strengthened.

– 21 –
A Singing, Laughing, Dancing Child

I saw in vision how a risen child sang, laughed and danced from one circle of color to the other. The child said to me:

I died early.
Very many children suffer and are not loved.
Bring them this song as a greeting from me.
Here, in the wonderful, beautiful life of heaven,
I can laugh, dance, and sing a lot,
even though I was ill on earth.

The child then danced from one patch of color to another and sang:

I sing, I praise, I dance and laugh,
I sing and praise and dance along.
I sing, I praise, I dance and laugh,
I sing and praise and dance along.
I sing, I praise, I dance and laugh,
I sing and praise and dance along.
I sing, I praise, I dance and laugh,
I sing and praise and dance along.

Peter, My Son

I would like to conclude this section with the words of my son Peter,
spoken twenty-three years after his death.

10.5.1988
Peter appeared, and around him were bright red-green flowers. There
followed a period of silence, and afterwards I saw him in the midst of
standing wheat bearing ripe, strong, healthy grain. He spoke:

I was born and grew up as a Christian among Christians.
I lived as a Christian.
I became linked with God consciously
from the example set by my father,
and became consciously aware of what it means to live in Christ
through the visions of my mother.
In this way I experienced the years of my growing up
as a Christian.

At an early age—twenty-three—
I left my earthly garment behind.
(*I saw in vision how, in a state of light, he left his body head first.*)
I kept a link with the earth and with the people,
as well as with the kingdom of heaven.

In spirit I lived as a figure of light on earth,
and yet away from the earth, above the earth.
You call it the universe.
The universe is greater than what has been accepted by science.
They will discover yet more distant galaxies.

So I was first of all a human being on earth,
then redeemed as a figure of light above the earth,
yet on the earth.
I rejoiced and felt great joy when I first saw the angels.
I was amazed that my mother had already seen all that!

She should paint more—for others!
Then I entered the realm of the saints.
Again I was full of joy.
Francis of Assisi looks just as my mother saw him.
Mary, the mother of Jesus Christ, is more loving,
and her colors of light are more beautiful—
the red crown, the blue staff, and a deep golden aura
all around her.
The edge around her garment of light is deep red.
Her face, her eyes, are bright—almost like a white light!

Messengers who serve are present in heaven.
Christ's presence is powerful,
and around him I saw the great figures of the Bible—
all in light.

I could see Peter cast his eyes toward Greece, Israel, and Ireland. There were patches of light and paths of light across the earth. He continued:

As I stood before Christ in silence and looked at him,
he moved his arms slowly
and with his right thumb blessed me,
making a cross of light on my forehead....

Then Christ spoke to me:
"Rejoice!
Live fully!
Serve God and your fellow humans
made in God's image and likeness.
Serve all creation!"

Christ blessed me with a large sign of the cross.
It was the length of my body.
And then he blessed me again
with a cross of light on my head.

Peter looked to me and spoke:

This is the way, this is life—after death.
Thus I live, love, and serve.

Risen people have a soul, a spirit, and a life in God.
A clothing of light in human form is around them.
The flowers and the wheat that you saw around me are symbolic.
They indicate growth and development of new life on earth.
You do not know this.
It is God-given life that we, Risen Ones, sow, guard, and guide.
God makes creation evolve.
Life grows and spreads out over the earth and in the universe
with our cooperation!

I wanted to tell you this,
so that you and other people may look forward to eternal life,
which is and remains in Christ, in God,
together with the Holy Spirit.
Amen.

They Searched for the Truth

Introduction

In 1991, Joa thought that her visionary experiences of the greater life after death were complete. The visions would be privately printed in the original German in 1995. The delay was due to the fact that, in 1991, her life changed. Her husband died, and she herself had to undergo a very serious operation. It was God's will that she recover. Her time had not yet come. There was still work to be done to complete her task on earth. Something was still missing, which the risen people of heaven had to communicate to her.

The visions in this section are concerned with men and women who seek to know the truth. The reality of death and the question of survival beyond life on earth are intrinsic to this quest. The search for ultimate meaning has always been in the domain of religion. Religious leaders from earlier levels of civilization possessed a primordial sensitivity for truth. The shamans are to be loved, respected, and encouraged in their path of development, here on earth as in heaven. In the afterlife, there are other individuals who can't accept the world contained in the Old and New Testament, who will struggle with it, and who may be helped to find their own way to it through the prayers of those who loved them on earth. Others have searched and discovered points of truth while on earth. In heaven, they stand amazed at the immense depth and complexity of the human soul and spirit. The Risen Ones tell us, over and over again, that truth cannot be fixed but is an ongoing process. The psyche must remain autonomous, yet not isolated from one's fellow human. The subjugation of others through the abuse of power prevents the spiritual unfolding of humankind. We are never to forget the magnitude of freedom contained in the faith and in God's love for humanity. In this way, we move forward in the full truth of evolving creation. Some Risen Ones discover a deeper significance of the Christian teachings unknown to them while on earth. A new creation has been made possible because of the events that occurred between Good Friday and Easter. Christ has truly risen and brought to humanity, not only how to live on earth in a healthy way, but also the unimaginable greatness of life after death. Once more the resurrection of the soul and spirit are described, but now the transformation of the human body into a risen body of light is included. This, according to the visions, is the truth of life, its full blossoming.

– 1 –
Shamanism

On the thirteenth of July 1996, I saw St. Luke in vision. He spoke to me:

Shamans, who are spiritual healers,
are still to be found among indigenous people
in the upper regions of the Northern hemisphere,
and in the South, in Africa.
Shamans possess a fine sensitivity for all living things—
for human beings, animals, and plants.
Primordial humanity had this kind of sensitivity
within themselves.

With the evolution of the mind
and a rational scientific approach to life,
we lost the primordial sensitivity.
Few people still possess this sensitivity
through hereditary transmission.

Shamans possess a capacity for psychic perception
that is not the same
as that which most European or American psychics possess.
Distinguish between fortune-telling and shamanism.
The foretelling of the future can even be a sin.
The primordial sensitivity of shamans
is a perception of a spiritual constellation,
even from a far distance.
Primordial humanity lived in this way.

I and others have personally experienced how shamans from all parts of the world perceive and respect people who are close to Christ and who are authentically related to God in a selfless way. St. Luke spoke again in an appealing way:

Let these people develop spiritually.
Give them enough time to do so.

Eighteen months later I discussed this chapter with a friend and questions arose about shamanism in South America and Australia. I went to pray in the Catholic church. There St. Francis appeared in vision and spoke:

I know the shamans.
You were told about shamanism
because it was a stage of development in humanity.
Had all humans been able to protect and maintain
their own "I"
then a religious unfolding from the shamanistic cultures
would have taken place.
But the development of technology—the technological mind—
and technical progress intervened (*as in the Iron Age*).
So Christ was given to the people of Israel for all humankind.

Then the human spirit and mind
advanced by leaps and bounds.
Grasp it if you can!
Abraham and Moses were not shamans.
Their spirit was in advance of the shamans.
Love the shamans!
In the southern parts of Africa shamans are still living.
The spirit of the Indians of South and North America
is highly developed.
There are true and authentic shamans
among the Aborigines of Australia.
They have preserved the wholeness of the human spirit.

– 2 –

The Testimony of My Friend Margrit

Margrit died on the 29th of June 1996. She was a Swiss woman with a powerful personality. She taught music and was a lover of nature. She sought the meaning of life in religion. She often traveled in the Orient and there encountered Buddhism. She practiced Buddhist meditation. She believed in the Christian understanding of love and she loved the Buddhist teachings on reincarnation—a process of birth, death, and rebirth culminating in the purity of the spirit. Because of her, I began to read The Tibetan Book of the Dead. *On reading this book, I understood spirit to be the ultimate reality in the Tibetan tradition. This tradition describes the spiritual self as being all-knowing, pure truth, empty—like the clarity of a cloudless sky. Gautama Buddha did not know of a personal God nor of a mediator between heaven and earth nor of a personal soul, as the Christian tradition understands it. The goal, presented in this book, is to achieve pure spirit, emptiness,*

Nirvana. In this conception there appears to be no God and no individual existence after death. Before she died, Margrit underwent a spiritual crisis. She did not want just to be a pure spirit after death. She wanted to live. She wanted to remain her individual self!

One day, I asked Mary why I could not see angels with Margrit? I usually saw angels in the presence of those who were dying. Mary, the mother of the Lord, looked earnest and answered:

She rejected us, who have risen from the dead.
She rejected Christ and the angels.
Thus we cannot reach her.
She pushes us away consciously.
Yet she will find a path to God and Christ.

A few days later Margrit died and on that same day an angel appeared to me and said:

She has died.
Protect her with the Our Father
and accompany her soul and spirit into Christ's kingdom—
into the life and work of the Risen Ones.

I prayed and in vision I saw Margrit, in the process of dying, calling out:

Buddha was a great man!
Christ is life!

Some hours later, a saint spoke:

You have prayed.
She is at rest and is earnest.
She will go on her path—a path of personal development.

On the next day in vision I saw Margrit, who had risen from the dead! Light surrounded her; the upper part of her body by a yellow light, the middle part by a blue light, the lower part by a green light, and the feet by a brown light. I had never seen colors in this way before. Then I saw a messenger of God speak to Margrit:

Listen!
Two people on earth
are creating a link with Christ for you through prayer.
May your spirit and soul be at peace.
God, through Christ, will give you
a new life of growth and development.
Ancestors who lived the Buddhist faith and who are now dead
and messengers of God are with you
and will help you live the new life after death, year by year.

Margrit then spoke about her long struggle with death:

I always thought I knew what is best for others;
that is spiritual pride, which I have now put aside.
I am now the same as others, one link in a long chain.
My great struggle in death
was to finally become who I am—
no longer above other human beings!

She spoke to me:

Write this down in the book of books!
There are many who wish to be above their fellow humans.
Thus they are stopped in their development
and thus no life flows into the soul!

One week later Margrit spoke again:

I believed that I was closer to true spiritual development
with Buddha's teachings on reincarnation.
I believed I understood more than the Hebrews and Christians.
I say to you now it was wrong to think I was superior.

The next day Margrit continued:

Listen!
I have been redeemed from the earth,
yet I am near the earth.
Please pray the Eucharist three times
during the next three months
so that I become a person of light, linked with Christ.

Some hours later:

I am alive!
I have cast away my earthly mantle.
I have the ancestors around me
and yet I see in the distance a field of light
in an area where the Risen Ones live.
I know my spirit will evolve further
so that I reach this field.
It is a great blossoming of soul and spirit
to be able to serve God as a human being.
After several cycles of the moon I will see Christ.

I don't yet have a relationship to the risen Christ,
nor to the angels or Mary.
Pray! Love God and your fellow human!
If you try to live united with Christ,
you will live in God's kingdom, you will live with God.

The Christian faith is the purest, strongest link with God,
the source of all life.

*The next day in church, Margrit appeared in vision and explained
many things:*

I am in human form—I see, hear, and speak.
I do not eat, nor do I need food.
My body exists out of a living energy of light,
as you explained to me on earth.
There is a force that holds the body together, like a magnet.
I cannot explain how this body has been made.
This body is held together by energy.
Believe it. I cannot explain it. It does not decompose.

*In prayer I saw Margrit absorbing the mystery of Mount Sinai. She
saw great fields of light on this mountain. She spoke again:*

I have already experienced Abraham!
It was a great period when Abraham lived.
Abraham was a man of great spirituality,

so great that I am astonished and ashamed
and wish to tell you that I had nothing
of the spiritual greatness of that man in me.

Now I am experiencing the period of Moses
and the mountain with the fields of light—
where the Ten Commandments came into existence.

I would like to dwell here a long time.
It was an important period in creation.

*On the seventeenth of July of that same year, I saw in vision Margrit
witnessing the formation of the Ten Commandments. This lasted
weeks. Moses, linked with God, wandered around the mountain. He
often sat down, in powerful union with God. The Ten Commandments fell like shadows onto the rocks. The power of light branded the
words into them. Margrit was pensive and said very seriously:*

The Ten Commandments remain even today
guidelines for us to behave rightly as human beings.

*Then Margrit saw a Bedouin tent in the Sinai desert. The next day
she spoke again to me:*

My capacity for discernment is still very brief and weak.
But I believe that Moses was one of those great people
to whom God has spoken and revealed himself!
Abraham was closer to me personally.
He was a strong and free individual, linked with God.
It was very important that he begot Ishmael and Isaac.
This was a great step forward in the evolution of humankind.

*Margrit saw in a rocky valley far away a small settlement full of light.
She spoke again:*

David who became king
came from a good family where there was much light. . . .
I have not yet worked through my experiences of Moses.
He was a pillar of light between heaven and earth.
People today have forgotten him. Why?

Then she said:

Read through the books of Moses again,
and pay attention to Abraham.
I am in a process of becoming a new person!

Two days later she spoke to me full of joy:

I am moving further on this first level of discernment,
away from the ancestors. I rejoice!
My friend Lotte would be happy!
The prophets are very great people!

*Nearly two weeks later, I saw in vision that Margrit had an angel by
her side for the first time. She looked at the angel and spoke:*

I am ashamed of my life.
Not everything I did was wrong,
many things had a cultural significance,
but love and the link of light from me to God was weak,
just not there.
Where did I make the first mistake?

I am just beginning to find and move on the path of love.
Pray for me.

*A week later, Margrit spoke to her father whom she saw far in the
distance:*

I am in the process of understanding memory
as a reliving of the past.

*She said this with great joy. On the next day, I saw that Margrit had
a Christian saint near her who would accompany her. He said to her:*

Do you understand the memory of the Jewish people?

Margrit smiled and replied:

In the last few days I have learned that memory means a reliving
of the past. A reliving of the past is to absorb lived experiences
within oneself and within one's soul. I do not have to memorize
the Hebrew scriptures—the Old Testament—and then the New

Testament. I must relive the life and history of the Hebrew
people! I must absorb their life in my soul!

Some time later she continued:

I am beginning to understand the spiritual development
of a people and a nation.
My spirit and my prayers have not yet reached God or Christ.
I am still in a process of becoming. I am grateful!
I have experienced the birth of light, Jesus.
The birth in a camel's stable was very simple;
heaven was open.
Angels were present. They came and they sang.
Saints too were there and an abundance of light was to be seen.
God's presence in spirit, life, and light was powerful.

The way you celebrate Christmas
in the church calendar is too weak.
You, Joa Bolendas, live with the birth of Christ,
where heaven and earth meet.
Live with God through Christ!

*I asked if Margrit's path of knowing Christ went further? An angel
answered:*

Yes, up to Pentecost.

– 3 –

The Earthquake of Kobe

*Just after the big earthquake in Japan, I saw in vision a man standing
in Kobe. Around him were a few doctors. The man spoke to me:*

Stand by us. We are moving through the valley of death.
Create for us a link with God, the primal spirit.

Speak about this to a friend of yours.
I am a doctor. He knows me.

I phoned my friend. He knew a doctor from Kobe who could have been the figure who appeared in vision.

– 4 –
A Famous Psychologist

In August 1995 I saw in vision a famous psychologist. I knew he had died in 1961. I saw him at the speaker's stand of a congress, which was being held in Zurich that August. From there he looked at the hundreds of psychologists present at the congress and began to speak seriously:

You have stood still and do not live in this day and age!
You heal evil from the past but let additional evil sow itself!
You don't intervene! Be men! Be women!
Help the peoples of the world live authentically!

In September he spoke again. Turning the pages of the Bible, he said:

In the beginning was the Word,
and the Word was formed as a living presence.
The human being, in soul and spirit,
stayed constantly linked with the core of creation,
consciously or unconsciously.
Today, in this period of strife,
soul and spirit are consciously seeking
the core of creation.
They search for God.

To me he said:

Many people, followers of Christ,
suffered, bore affliction, underwent martyrdom.

Today, at the turn of the millennium,
there will be no martyrs,
but men and women of strength will dare something new.

Some days later, now risen from the dead, he spoke again:

Hold on to religion as the highest principle.
It is important to know about the evolution of humankind.
Psychology is a branch of knowledge
that helps people be conscious.
But to be religious is to live as a human being
in the entirety of creation.
Moving and being moved
by the spirit of one's fellow human
is a truly human experience.
The Sermon on the Mount from the New Testament
moves the spirit of men and women in a timeless way.
Revelation moves the human spirit with light and energy.

Here I asked him if he was talking about John's Revelation in the New Testament? He answered:

Yes and no. It is not solely about John's Revelation.
Every authentic revelation in religion
contains light from God, from the core of creation.

Then he was pensive and spoke again:

It is dangerous when psychologists today
bind others to themselves too intensively
and then release them.
A healthy psyche must not cut itself off
from another human being.
The psyche remains autonomous
but not separate from others.
I speak about soul and spirit,
not about sexual bonding, as in marriage.
In marriage, bonding and the maintaining of a community
are necessary and provide rootedness.

My wife, my children, and my grandchildren
were important to me and for my life in general.
They gave me light and energy
for the presence of my spirit on earth.

Once again he said:

It is not right
when psychologists create very powerful bonds
between people and then abruptly dissolve them.
This is important. Write it down.
Now look very carefully.

Then I saw this famous man as he was on earth. I looked a second time and I saw him transformed into a figure of light in the same human form! Then there was stillness. The vision of transfiguration was powerful and I slowly uttered the following words in prayer. "I give thanks that I could witness all of this. I ask Jesus to stand by me so that I may experience the creation of this book in a way that is authentic and relevant to this day and age."

On the 28th of June 1996, a son of this man died. My husband knew him, so I started to pray for the son. While in prayer, I saw in vision that he could already see his father in the next world. A great deal of light, in dark violet and red colors, surrounded his father. I had never seen these kinds of colors around a risen person before. The son was astonished because he could see his father and even more because so much light was around him and in him. In a state of excitement, he said to his father:

You?
You.
Father?
Do you have so much light in you?
You have that?

The father laughed and answered:

I had a hard shell.

The son replied:

I am happy!
Now I know you ... your soul and spirit!
You were often very severe on earth!

The father continued:

I had many gifts from God—particles of knowledge—
therefore the hard shell.
I saw and knew more and tried to bring it into life.

Then he spoke to his son slowly:

I "saw" the past of human beings like a film.
The soul and spirit of men and women
are far more complicated than is known to psychologists.
The network of threads of the spirit is vast
and belongs to the truth of human nature.
What I discovered as a psychologist is only a small point
in the creative activity of the world of spirit.
The human being lives in the midst of creation.
Men and women are surrounded
by countless creative impulses
in a vast area which is part
of the totality of God's creation.
The sun, moon and stars are to be seen in this area.

He spoke to his son again slowly and joyfully:

In this vast realm of creation,
I, as a human on earth, saw something of the human psyche ...
only a small point in all this immensity. ...
You, my son, will experience, see, hear many things,
serving and working together with me in creation,
when the time is ready.
After several moons you will see Christ.

On the next day I checked over all that I had seen. My son, Peter, in heaven added:

It is true.
This man possessed much light
and special cell membranes when he lived on earth.
Now he lives in the greater life.
His life was and is more intense than others.
He was not a Peter, a Paul, or a John
but he was chosen by God to "see" more into human nature.
Now, in the afterlife, he sees a whole section of creation.
When he has taken in this level of being over years,
we will meet each other.
You are to go on your path in peace and confidence.

A well-known and close colleague of this famous psychologist died in 1998. I only saw a small section of a meeting between them in the hereafter. Both were involved in a serious discussion. I heard the famous psychologist say:

Now from here, from the true life of the spirit,
we see how important our work on earth was for humanity.
You see also the mistakes we made!

The colleague answered in the same earnest manner:

Love! We did not research love
from a depth-psychological perspective.

– 5 –

My Brother

Sometime in January 1996 an angel appeared in my visions and said:

When your brother Willhelm dies, angels will be with him,
as well as Mary, the mother of the Lord,
and a Greek saint called Ariop.

On the February 17 of that year, my brother became ill with a severe flu. I prayed for him and an angel answered:

Pray twelve rosaries for him.
He will have an easy death, will rise from the dead,
and will see his father in the hereafter.
He will also "see" his five children, his grandchildren,
and his wife, Ilse,
who are still living with you on earth.
He will be happy. Later he will "see" you on earth.
Joy and peace shall be within him.

On this day I could already see in vision that two days after his death, our mother would be near him, but that he would not be able to see her.

Five days later Willhelm died. I prayed and Otto, my departed husband, said to me in vision:

Give thanks that he could die.
He has already risen from the dead
and can see the world of angels.
In three days, he will see you all.
Do not weep, his life has been fulfilled.
He was a strong and important man on earth.
He was linked with God, more than you realize.

After these words, I remembered that my brother was religious in his own way. He followed the teachings of Rudolf Steiner and was an Anthroposophist. Two days later, Peter, my son who died many years ago, appeared and spoke:

Willhelm is loved and he will meet us and others in heaven!

Peter continued joyfully:

Then a new dimension will come into your life!

The next day, Peter spoke again:

Your brother has seen a path of light.
He was full of joy, looked around and said:

I believe I am entering a life of light,
the one that John the Evangelist saw.

Willhelm then appeared in my vision and said:

I see an angel.

The angel nodded, confirming Willhelm's statement.
Willhelm continued:

That means that I have now reached
the beginning of a new development.

Willhelm was amazed and awaited what would happen next. He
spoke again:

I believe that my sister, Joa,
does not know this level of development.

He then turned to the angel:

May I speak so that my sister can see and hear me?
Then she can tell my other sister, Margaretha,
and my own family all that she has seen and heard.

The angel nodded again and Willhelm continued:

Good. I want to speak but I can't see the earth yet.

The angel, with blue radiant light around its yellow illuminated body,
nodded again, and my brother continued:

I was half asleep, not quite awake.
When I became fully awake,
I was aware that my body had been totally infused with spirit.
I had a body full of energy, full of spirit,
that was tangible and could move.
In the language of science: it was a body
of elementary particles of matter with an atomic structure,
similar in fashion to bodies on earth and in the universe.
I remain I, and yet I am different.
It is true that the entirety of creation
comes from the same matter.

I am I, only the matter that is mine
is put together in another way,
similar to the way I would live on earth as a human being,
yet I am transformed.
Perhaps I can explain it better later on.
The understanding and transformation of matter
has been a sublime experience for me.

Slowly:

But it is possible to grasp and understand all of this....
Silence.
Now I see the earth in the far distance—a blue sphere.
I see Joa, and our other sister Margaretha and her family.
I see them! I really see them!

The angel spoke to Willhelm:

In the next few days you will see your own family and friends.
We have now given you a time for further development.
Amen.

I asked my brother where all the Risen Ones live. He thought about this and said:

Not in a cloud of light as many of you believe.
I can't explain it yet.
Certainly we live near the earth, the moon, and the sun.
This is for you a great distance but for us only a small one.
Guard the earth with your soul and spirit.
It is the greatest and most evolved
of God's creations at this time.

That afternoon, Willhelm spoke again:

I see the realm of heaven with angels and risen saints!

And the angel spoke to Willhelm:

In three months you will be with the saints—with the Risen Ones!

Two days later, Willhelm appeared in vision, looked at me, and said:

Heaven and earth touch each other and form a unity of spirit—
all in the unity of God's creation. Do you understand this?
Love God's creation, earth,
love it as a unit in the radiance of the spirit.
You do not know this.
The universe is in a process of becoming.
Our earth is the most evolved creation in the universe.
Pray for it. It is in danger of being weakened by human hands.

On the second of March that same year, Willhelm spoke again:

Write this down!
The life that begins after the transformation
into a risen human being is the true life.
Men and women then live
in the final magnificent blossoming of their lives!
Do not be afraid of it!
I experience it with great joy, and know
that you too will experience it in this way.

Slowly:

God's creation is vast, immense, and, without doubt,
can never be fully grasped!
I will tell you more later. Clouds hold water for the earth.
They protect against the sun and against the cold.
The sun will continue to exist for billions of years.
It is important to give thanks for this!

I asked Willhelm about the danger from a hole in the ozone layer, He answered:

Speak about the holes in the ozone layer.
There are already several.
Pray. Pray often, for the holes in the ozone layer
are a great danger for the earth.
Rays of the sun are not the only danger for earth.
Rays from the whole of outer space can enter the atmosphere!

The balance of oxygen in the atmosphere can change.
Nevertheless the earth with humankind will remain.
There can only be disturbances—that is God's will.
Remain in prayer before God for the earth.

Then Willhelm saw and heard angels singing. He looked at them a long time and said to me:

It is the first time that I see and hear how angels sing!
They sing in a more conscious and solemn way than you on earth.
Wonderful....

Then he repeated this in a more gentle voice:

Wonderful....
to see and hear all this.

On Good Friday of that year, Willhelm spoke again:

This is the first time that I see the mystery of Good Friday.
Christ died on the cross and was visible to all.
He would have died at that time, even if in another manner.
His death and resurrection were consummated at that time.
The time could not be deferred.
What Christ made new within God's creation
is what you experienced in earlier visions.
It is the plan of creation that a human being
—every human being—live in the hereafter
on the same day that he dies.
Yes, human becoming continues,
the final magnificent blossoming in the greater life.

Willhelm looked at me seriously and said:

In the stillness of death—
from Good Friday to the Easter morning—
a bright light of great intensity was present.
The light was almost white and of a rare quality.
A great thing had happened. I will never be able to grasp it.
I am astonished and filled with joy.
Love this period!

This time—between Good Friday and Easter—heals much pain,
and can also heal sickness in many people.

Slowly:

During these days,
Through Christ,
prayer and the work of medical doctors
can open the doors of healing. Give thanks!

I remembered that Willhelm had wanted to become a doctor. It was therefore important for him to experience this kind of healing. A week later the visions continued and he spoke again:

I see so many people on earth who are in a mad rush
and who live without any spiritual meaning.
Pray for those thousands, millions of human beings,
that the new spirit of the age will reach them.
Much light is visible in South Africa.
Here are people whose soul and spirit
are capable of absorbing spiritual life from God.
The same is visible in parts of Portugal,
south Sweden, and Mongolia.
Go now and write it all down.

Four days later, I could see Willhelm in vision beside the baptismal font in the Protestant church at Küsnacht. He said:

Pray now for the people on earth.

I prayed. Then he said:

Pray to God that there may be peace
in the hearts of humankind.

I prayed. And he said:

Pray that the heavens do not become red and darken.

I prayed.

One week later, Willhelm appeared again and began to speak to me:

As a risen man, I have entered the animal kingdom.
Take your time to come with me.
The world of animals is the stage preceding human evolution.
The human being with all his or her natural inclinations,
with spirit, and with the ability to connect with God's Spirit,
which is primal, remains the crown of creation.

Listen! The evolution of the animal is God's creation.
Look at the plants and the animal world before humankind.
It was a wonderful period of creation.
They lived and loved each other—
the animals, the flowers, the plants.
You just cannot understand how peaceful
this preceding stage of human evolution was.
This was a preliminary stage, not more.
Humans need the plants, not the animals, as food to survive.

Write down: In the process of creation,
the animal world is a prior stage of evolution
for human development.
This took place over millions of years.
God engaged a section of creation to create a human being.
With a new cell, God created the human being
in the body of an animal, which had human resemblance!

Love the animals, protect the animals,
even though they are no longer necessary for the survival of life.
Humans can live without the animals,
but they serve you in many different ways.
Give thanks for them.

On Easter Monday of that year, Willhelm spoke to me again:

Rejoice!
Christ has truly risen, as has been written by Luke!
Rejoice that you have completed your work!
Write about how you have experienced these things!

Slowly:

I know that you have heard and seen the truth.
Christ lives!
What I have seen and understand up to now
is that Christ abides near God, spiritually in God.
I believe I will never grasp or come to know
the greater heavenly realm that lies in the beyond.
But I do believe a task is ready for me
in the heaven of the angels and saints.
The task will be given to me
so that I can be active and help on earth.
Life on earth is still in a process of becoming—
so much is done without love.

The spirit of Africa must be rescued,
otherwise it will fall under false expectations
brought about by capitalism.
China too must not die spiritually.
China needs three thousand years for its spiritual transformation.
India needs love.
Many peoples of the earth need love.
Pray. You will create spiritual links for humankind
through prayer. Amen.

On the eleventh of May 1996, I asked my brother if he could tell me
more exactly about anthroposophy? I asked this because I knew that
Willhelm was an anthroposophist. In my vision, he became serious and
said:

I have seen many things.
I have experienced many things,
but I have not absorbed everything.
That will take years.
What I have experienced up to now is your world
and the development of the earth.
It is the truth, therefore write your books.
Rudolf Steiner was a great man who sought the truth.
He recognized many things. Look at his childhood.

*I remembered that Rudolf Steiner grew up in a Catholic family with
a strong and solid faith. Willhelm continued:*

While he was a student,
he broke away from the security of his childhood.
He sought freedom. He remained a Christian.
He only rejected the many dogmas and power in the church,
so that he could reflect about religion and human nature
in a new way.
I assume that his belief about the seven-year stages
of human development was nothing more than a help
to understand human maturation,
as I now see it.

He tried to find the life of Christ
without the teachings of the church.
He felt and sought for the true Christ.
He had a presentiment of the great mystery—
of Christ's link with the core of creation, with God.
Rudolf Steiner "saw" the earth's evolution
up to modern man and woman.
A trust in Christ and God, that is born out of freedom,
enables the human being to meet Christ,
the Holy Spirit, and God,
who is primal.
And through this blossoming of the spirit,
men and women become beings of light.

Willhelm added:

Steiner was concerned with the entirety of human development.
He saw the possibility of development for every human,
including the mentally handicapped.
This was his essential achievement.

*Just before Pentecost of that year, Willhelm spoke again. During this
vision, I was praying in the church of Einsiedeln. Willhelm looked
around the large church, and then spoke in an earnest way:*

Avoid power in the church,
avoid the misuse of power in the Catholic faith.
From this church, accept everything
that unites men and women with God
in the new unity of religions.
Do the same with the Orthodox Church.
From the Evangelical Church of Luther,
accept the Bible as valid for all humankind,
the love of your neighbor, and human rights
for all peoples of the earth.
From the Jewish faith, accept the basic laws
that are valid for humankind,
as in the Ten Commandments.
You are to affirm their trust in God,
as witnessed in the great figures of the Old Testament.

In vision I could see the Pentecostal flame above the heads of all my friends. It was especially bright and strong in the community of a Swiss convent. On Pentecost Sunday, Willhelm spoke again:

Pentecost! A great feast to experience here in heaven.
Open your eyes!
Christ, as a figure of light, shows us the energies of creation
that come from God to the universe,
to the sun, the moon, and the stars,
reaching the earth in a powerful way.
The active power of the Holy Spirit,
which moves the universe and the earth,
is different from the Holy Spirit's influence on human beings.
Hold on to this: the unity of God, the Holy Spirit,
and humankind!

Listen! The ecumenical circle will be completed
when humans have recognized the true religion.
This involves an evolution of the peoples of the world.

Neither nationality, the Eastern Orthodox Church,
the Roman church, the faith of Israel,
nor the Protestant churches of the North are decisive,

even though the adherence to a tradition
is understandable from a psychological perspective.
Only the truth about Christ and God,
creator of heaven and earth, is what counts.
Work on this!

In vision Rudolf Steiner now spoke:

Be awake! Examine everything in prayer,
whenever there are discussions!
Hold on to the great link of human beings with God,
who continually sustains primal creation.
All life of the spirit comes from primal creation,
and this will always be so!

Willhelm spoke once more:

Listen to me carefully!
Nuclear science has discovered elementary particles of matter—
the atom, the electron, nuclear particles, quarks....
There are five further components.
Science will yet explore three of them.
Science will anticipate and explore only in part the fourth particle.
Humans will not be able to explain the final component of matter,
the fifth particle.
This point of God's continuous creation
remains a mystery for us human beings.
Listen! How elementary particles of matter become
a tree, a stone, a living being is God's creation.
God's Spirit and God's light give us humans
our life on earth and our life in the kingdom of heaven.
God created the human being with light and with the Holy Spirit
with elementary particles of matter.
God created the human being in his image and likeness.
This remains a mystery of God's creation.

*Two years later (January 24, 1998), when these visions were being
translated, I was asked about the statement: "matter being put together
in another way" in the risen human being. As I prayed about this, a*

saint appeared. He called himself St. Christopher and was sent from God. He began to speak:

Do not be afraid.
The atom is made up of energy.
The human soul and spirit are without atoms.
A risen human consists of a finer energy, soul, and spirit.
Spirit was in primal creation at the beginning. God is spirit.

Listen well: God first created energy,
before the creation of the universe.
The basic matter and the basic energy
of the universe is—the atom!

God gave breath, and spirit entered creation—
the beginnings of life.
God gave human beings a soul as a vessel, a center,
in which the Holy Spirit may dwell.
The brain is the instrument of the spirit.
Grasp whoever may grasp this. Amen.

One week later, an angel appeared saying:

I will help you with this question. Pray the "Our Father."

My risen son Peter explained.

Whether you find an atom
in earth, wood, stone, water, plants, or the living body,
the fundamental energy is always the same.
In God's creation, the human being exists out of a body of atoms
and a soul and spirit without atoms.
When the human dies, the atoms of the physical body fall away,
but a body of light energy remains,
together with soul and spirit.
After the transformation to a body of atoms of light energy,
the soul and spirit become more powerful.

I wondered whether I had understood rightly that the risen human has a garment in human form out of atoms of light energy. Mary answered:

Yes.

*I asked whether the human soul and spirit that are without atoms and
that are in relationship with Christ contain within them the life of
creation. Mary answered:*

Yes. Hold on to this truth! Do not ask more.
Atoms are God's creation.

*A week later there were more questions. Why are the waves of light
energy of the risen people invisible? An angel appeared and helped me.
The angel explained to me that the wavelengths of risen humans are
different from the normal light waves of the atom. They are finer and
fainter. There was another question about the unity of the risen human
being. The angel again showed me the unity of soul, spirit, and atoms
of light energy in the risen human. The light energy appeared as a fine
covering of the soul and spirit of the risen human, similar in form to
the physical body, when on earth. The angel spoke:*

The creation of the human spirit, soul,
and risen "body of atoms of light energy"
is a far greater creation than you can understand.

*That week I went again to church and prayed. Once again Peter,
together with three risen saints, appeared and said:*

Stay with this statement:
God created the atom, the universe, and the human being.
The energy of the atom is the fundamental energy
of creation and of the entire universe.
God created the human being
culminating with the development of the brain.
God gave a soul with a human spirit
only to the human being.
Through the process of evolution,
God made it possible
for human beings to enter into relationship
with the core of creation—with God.
When the earthly covering of the human being dies,
there remains soul and spirit,

which are without atoms,
in the form of a human body.
This body, the covering of the risen human,
consists of atoms of light energy.
Angels have this kind of body.
The light energy of this body is subtle, fine,
hardly visible, hardly measurable.
The light energy of the body of Christ is stronger,
as Paul witnessed on the road to Damascus.
This light energy—the inner- and outermost part of the atom—
is not known to you. For example,
you have angels around you and you do not see them.
The earth is surrounded by a fine, delicate layer
of atoms of light energy
that you do not see and cannot measure.
Listen: If this layer of light energy around the earth
did not exist, the magnificent blossoming of creation
would not have been possible!
Listen! A planet of another star needs to be surrounded
by such an invisible layer of light energy
so that its evolution becomes possible.
It needs this covering to receive informative patterns from God.
God gave your sun a clothing of atoms of light energy.
This covering contains the sun's warmth and heat
so that they remain subject to the processes of creation.
That is why your prayers for the sun, the moon and the stars
are important.
All things—the trees, stones, animals, humans—
have this fine covering around them
to receive messages from God.
All beings have the energy of creation within them.
The prayers of men and women move the energy of creation.
Prayer creates a spiritual union between God and creation.
The power of prayer brings into movement the link
between God and God's creation, earth.
What more do you want to know?
The earth will survive as it is now for many millions of years!

These visions were very powerful for me and hard to understand. I believe I "saw" the different levels of creation: primal creation and the world of spirit, the creation of the energy of the atom, the creation of the universe with all the stars and planets, the creation of life, the creation of the human soul and spirit, the creation of the brain. The human being is a wonderful unity of the different realities of God's creation. At death, the earthly clothing falls away. From the visions I do not know if this ultimate particle of matter is a substance, an energy, or a field. All I know is that the ultimate component touches the innermost and outermost part of matter and does not seem to be limited to our concepts of time and space, and is finally an impulse from the source of all being—God. A body of light energy together with soul and spirit lives on. As I was pondering on all this, another saint appeared:

Learn from this:
The more pure and conscious the link with God,
the stronger the power of the human spirit and human life!
All this through Christ!

After I had written this vision down, I "saw" many monks and theologians—Catholic, Orthodox, Protestant, women, and some scientists—standing in the choir of the Reformed church in Küsnacht. They lowered their heads as a sign of thanksgiving and praise. The whole choir was full of light and the words of an angel came forth:

Men and women—humanity—with Christ,
joined with God:
this ... is ... the ... church!

Finally, after this powerful vision, Christ appeared in the full radiance of light.

He spoke slowly and earnestly:

Creation is the primal source of life.
I came from the primal source.
Do you understand this in all its greatness?

Thus ends this section of visions on my brother Willhelm, and others. I would like to add that Rudolf Steiner first appeared in vision in 1994.

At that time he made comments on the visions of the philosophy professor, published in this book, and regretted that the philosophers have not yet recognized the spirit of St. John. Together with the professor, he called upon humankind to live the new freedom of the spirit and live the love for one's fellow human being. In this way only can there be an unfolding and blossoming of the human spirit.

A New Creation

Introduction

Once again, Joa thought that her work on the Risen Ones was complete. The above section was privately printed in 1996. The following year Susanna, a friend of Joa, died. Risen from the dead, she wanted Joa to pass on more of the visions about the immense implication of Christ's resurrection, uniting heaven and earth into a new whole, and thus bringing about a new creation.

Joa had witnessed this process in visions on the life of Moses. Moses sought and found unity with God. Thus he lived in God's world and in the ongoing process of creation. Moses can still participate in the processes of ongoing creation today, because he found unity with God. His spirit is alive in God and thus he can move and enlighten human beings. His spirit can move, guide, and enlighten those who seek his help. According to the testimony of Joa, it is possible to experience Moses on Mount Sinai and at the Wailing Wall of Jerusalem. This is otherwise with Ramses II. Joa witnessed Ramses as being a great man. Although he was a powerful figure with much goodness and wisdom, he did not live in unity with God. Therefore his powerful energies have remained dormant in the afterlife. Prayer is needed to release this powerful figure from the stiffness of death. Through prayer and supplication, Ramses will connect to God, Christ, and the Holy Spirit and, as one risen from the dead, the energies of this great ruler will be released and made available for humankind. Joa could foresee that the powerful, wise, and healing influence of Ramses would be felt in areas known to him during his lifetime. She had also to pray for the ancient empress of northern China and for a Russian princess, Olga. These two figures were immensely important for the lands where they lived and ruled. They too needed to be released from the stiffness of death. Their energies will influence men and women of today in a positive way, and thus these great figures of the past can participate in the expansion of creation and in the development of the human being.

What has been promised? What has been offered for the future development of human society here on earth?

Today men and women are unsure about the future of human life. They have become skeptical of the many promises for a better society, world peace, and economic expansion that are offered by politicians of our times. Threats of war, nuclear devastation, the destruction of nature, dwindling natural resources, climatic changes, growing world population, new diseases, mass unemployment, the increasing gap between the rich and the poor seem to undo the optimistic schemes proposed by well-intentioned individuals, institutions and governments. At times it seems that the earth itself has become unhinged from its axis and humanity has lost its way. The uncertainty of the future fills men and women with fear. We no longer trust our leaders and human hands to lead us out of the present dark night of civilization.

In this age of doubt and uncertainty, the call for spirit should not be ignored. Spirit is at the core of our nature. A life without spirit is a life caught in the stiffness of death. All too often in our history, spirit has been understood in an abstract way as transcending, even sometimes denying, the experiences of life on earth. The visions presented here are in their very essence life affirming. Spirit is understood as expressing the meaning and transformation of life experiences on earth, so that they come to their full truth in the light of God and of eternal life.

The visions of Joa Bolendas tell us that the highest development of the human spirit is its linking with God's Spirit. In various ways, the visions amplify this development in the lives and works of the prophets of the Old Testament, Jesus Christ, and those saints and holy people who have risen from the dead. They all live in unity with God. As risen from the dead, they are connected to a totality that embraces the Alpha and Omega of existence. Yet they also contain within themselves experiences from their lives on earth. These figures are full of wisdom and farsightedness. In their lives on earth and even more so in heaven, they recognize truth, goodness and beauty. They see God's world here on earth as well as in heaven. According to this testimony, we on earth can already belong to the community of Risen Ones. Together with them we can make available an enormous storehouse of spiritual energy to guide the future of humankind, to restore the earth to its axis, and to inspire men and women, institutions and governments to make the right decisions that will help improve human life on earth in both its material and spiritual dimensions.

As part of this linking process, we are to find ways of restoring the significance of prayer. We are to learn to pray to God so that our ancestors may be relieved from the stiffness of death. Our prayers are to bring about the unity between the living and the dead. Living in the unity of God, the Risen Ones, and our fellow humans on earth, we can create a better world, not just one of material satisfaction but one with more meaning and more love. Prayer connects us with God's intentions for life on earth, and according to these visions, those intentions are to break the power of death and to prepare men and women to be truly alive in God's world, now and in the hereafter. Joa Bolendas' visions testify to the fullness of a new creation that came into being between Good Friday and Easter Sunday.

– 1 –
Moses

15.2.1997
Mary said to me:

The great crisis in the churches is coming.
You will overcome it. A new period will begin. Work!

A friend will bring to your work much knowledge of the spirit.
It is God's will. He will stand as a strong tree in the desert.
The desert is the spiritual emptiness of the present time.

Nicholas of Flue, a patron saint of Switzerland, spoke slowly:

I baptize him and anoint him with oil.
He will go to the mountain of Moses
and let himself be formed by God.

I asked when, how, where is the mountain? Nicholas answered:

It is possible at an altar in his home.
It is also possible in a church.
Let him do it two to three times a week.
He will find the way.

Later an angel said:

The best would be that he goes to Mount Sinai.

Once my friend decided to go to Mount Sinai, as part of a trip to Israel, I could hear in vision Nicholas of Flue:

There are signs of collapse in all the churches.
You and your small circle of friends are to stay calm.
Have courage to stand and speak when you are required to do so.
The earth trembles, the veil of the temple is torn.
Death is present, but also the resurrection into a new era!
It is good for all humanity that one of your friends
goes to Mount Sinai, there to meet God.

Another Risen One said:

Let your friend blow on a horn!
It is a call to battle!
After prayer on Mount Sinai, the golden calf will be defeated
—in Rome, in the churches of the East, in Constantinople.
This is symbolic, but speaks about the truth!

Easter 1997
A Risen One spoke, after my friend left for Mount Sinai:

He will return with joy. He was close to Moses and Christ.
He will write down his experiences,
place them on a small altar of light,
and then go back to a bench in the church to pray.

*In vision I could see much light around my friend as he prayed on
Mount Sinai. The whole upper part of the mountain was covered in
light. Angels, saints, and the power of the Holy Spirit were present. A
holy man of Israel spoke:*

In this way, the spiritual life of Israel and Christians can be saved.
His prayers have been heard! A new beginning for him!

*When my friend returned, we went to the church, prayed and gave
thanks. In vision I could see St. Paul standing by the Damascus gate
in Jerusalem. He spoke:*

I protect and fight for Israel!

The true story of St. Catherine of Alexandria
is that her dead body was stolen
and secretly brought to the mountain of Moses.
On this mountain,
Catherine can be seen as a figure of light
by some holy people.
Many people can feel her spiritual presence.
She connects people to the light
and works for the spiritual life
brought by Moses
and later by Jesus and his disciples.

She is an important saint
in the circle of Jesus' disciples in the greater life.
Accept her.

*About a week later, as I was praying for Israel, I saw Moses in vision.
He was full of strength and power as he stood high up on the mountain.
He was fighting a spiritual battle. From a distance, I could hear him
talking with God. I could hear the following:*

Love the prayers of Joa's friend.
Israel must not burn!
Israel must not be destroyed!

*And then I could hear him saying to himself that in five days the battle
would be over. On the next day, as I was in prayer, I saw in vision
huge clouds over Mount Sinai. I heard sounds of thunder. Moses was
speaking with God. I heard Moses saying "Shalom." I continued to
pray over the day and during the night. Gradually the thunder grew
less. I saw a bright pillar of light reaching up from Mount Sinai to the
heavens. Toward midnight it became a fine silver ray of light. On the
next day, as I prayed, I could see that all was still on the mountain of
Moses. No clouds, no thunder, no ray of light could be seen. I believed
something great had happened.*

One year later, I heard the voice of a risen saint:

Listen!

*And I saw in vision Moses. He stood on Mount Sinai and was clothed
in a bright robe of light. He looked at me very earnestly and said:*

Shape the Ten Commandments into Ten Prayers of Petition!
Help your friend Peter Barcaba, the composer,
to weave them into musical rhythm.
A great task for him!
Read Deuteronomy 5:1–22.

Moses continued:

What would happen if an Israeli woman
would pray the Ten Commandments in this new way?

I answered that she would gain a Christian attitude. Moses spoke again:

It would be the bridge for the Israelis
to proceed on their path of development!

What you have received about the Ten Commandments is correct.
The next commandment that follows
is the commandment of love.
Remember the words of Luke:
"You are to love the Lord your God with all your heart,
with all your soul, with all your strength, and with all your mind,
and your neighbor as yourself."
And therefore if you love God, you love Christ!

I asked: "If you love Christ, you love God?" Moses answered:

If you love God, you love Christ!
It is important to know this!

Some months later, a saint explained further:

The words from God to Moses, to human beings began with:
"You shall ... " "You shall not ... "
Through the link with Christ,
the commandment became a petition:
"I ask you, Jesus Christ, with the help of the Holy Spirit,
that I do not ... "
The "Our Father" is also a prayer of petition.

Have you understood?
Moses brought the commandments;
Christ brought the link with God for all humanity.

Ramses II

A saint spoke to me:

Listen!
Abraham, Moses, Joshua, Elijah, and others
maintained a spiritual relationship with God
while on earth and continue to live in heaven
as spiritual influences for the earth and humanity.
Ramses II, and others that you have witnessed in vision,
such as the empress of China and Mongolia,
once lived on earth, and now live in the hereafter,
but have not yet experienced the union of light with God.
A life in union with light is given to the dead;
a life that comes through Christ and prayer,
linking men and women with God.
In this way light energy of the spirit is set free,
and humans evolve
to become risen beings living in union with God.
We ask that people who are close to you
may go to the grave of Ramses II
to pray for the light of Christ.

My son and later another relative of mine visited the grave of Ram-
ses II. All of us who remained at home began to pray for Ramses II.
In October 1997, an angel gave us a prayer for this occasion:

Come and worship!
O God, creator of heaven and earth,
you gave us your son, the one son, Jesus Christ,
who gives us life, from Your Life,
for all creation on earth.
You gave us Christ who is active through his life-bringing light
and through the Holy Spirit.

We ask that, when prayers are said
at the grave of Ramses II,
light from God, Christ, and the Holy Spirit may be given.
We ask that the energy of creation
enters Ramses II and lives in him;
thus, in union with God, he may develop further
and live as a great spiritual influence,
for God, for humanity, for all creation on earth!

God, Jesus Christ!
We ask for Ramses II
that he receives life, and may be active
in the magnificent world of light and energy.

Amen.

*One week later, I saw, in vision, light, much light, being given to the
soul and spirit of Ramses II. On that same day, my relative visited the
Egyptian museum in Cairo and stood before the mummy of Ramses II.
We had planned to pray together on another day, when my relative
would have visited Ramses' grave. Her itinerary was changed, and
unexpectedly she could visit the museum. I understood the synchronicity
of my vision with her visit to the museum on the same day as a sign
of confirmation.*

*One week later, toward the end of October, a saint from Egypt
commented on this event:*

Thus the life energy in Ramses II has become free.
He is awakened and alive!
Give thanks to God for this!
Ramses II was not dead,
but his life energy was held back.

Great was my joy! As I was in prayer, John the Evangelist spoke to me:

Try to understand the levels of your joy.
The great life after death
that you witnessed in Ramses II
was a powerful experience, unknown to you.

And meditate on this:
God was gracious and let Ramses II develop further
to become what he perceives from God through Christ.
In this way he can be active for the Eastern part of the earth,
and for the spiritual development of Greece.

In the evening of that same day, I saw in vision Ramses II looking into the distance. He began to speak:

I have heard that in three weeks
my spirit will see and hear into the new period.

A saint added:

Ramses II does not have to experience his life
since the first day of his birth!
He must move on further,
joined with God, Christ, and the Holy Spirit.
In this way new strength will manifest in his prayer!

Then, in answer to our prayers for the Chinese empress, whom I knew from earlier visions, a saint spoke:

She has been freed so that she can experience energy from Christ.
Thank you for your prayers.
Light is visible throughout the northern part of China,
Mongolia, and in the north of Japan!

Later, Ramses spoke about what he had received and what he had understood about the spiritual evolution of humankind:

There was a period of development through Moses
who was the great spiritual leader of the people of Israel.
There are three parts to this development.
The first part: the coming into relationship with God—
the meeting with God on Sinai.
The second part concerns God's relationship with Israel
up to the time of Isaiah.
The third period extends far beyond Isaiah and the prophets,
up to and beyond Pentecost.

Abraham was and remains still today
a powerful link of light with God
for the people of the Nile, for Israel, and for the Arabs.

Pensively, Ramses continued:

Abraham's sons were lifelong friends and true brothers.
This continued until the fifth generation.
Leaders of the clans and warlords then divided the peoples
into Arabs and Israelis.

Then, after a stillness:

Over all this length of time these people
have not yet recognized their spiritual leaders,
such as Moses, Abraham, and others.

Stillness. Then:

Moses too lives in the present time.
He also has developed further.
Moses helps people today!
Open your eyes to the development of humankind!

I now saw Ramses II sit down on a large rock. He looked far, far across a desert landscape. After a long pause, he spoke to himself in a thoughtful and peaceful way:

God has shown me the development of humanity
up to this point.
Great things have been accomplished
from the period in which I lived up to the time of Isaiah!
A great step in evolution!
Evil and traumas were there too! I will put them aside;
I don't understand them.
What I anticipate is far away, behind many sand hills—
a bright light, like a star, in Jerusalem.
O God stand by me.

On the ninth of November of that same year, I saw in vision Ramses II looking at my first book, and having understood its contents, he looked all around and said:

This time will be dangerous!
The world burns!
If there is a God of Israel,
I now implore this God to extinguish the fire.

He continued seriously:

My soul and my spirit
are now in a process of discerning the period of Isaiah!
I want to understand! Pray for me.

After a moment's silence, he continued:

I am not Moses. He was, and still is, a chosen one!
I am amazed that the people on earth do not speak to him,
do not ask for help! Why?

Then, with a certain hesitation, he finally said:

I will try to find, in spirit, a path to him, a link with him.

On the twenty-eighth of November, I heard the following words far away:

I am Ramses II.
Please pray for me, pray for us.
I have gone through the great period of Isaiah.
I have lived through and prayed through this period before God
for the people of my time and for the whole land of Egypt.

A bright wall of light stands in front of me.
A king has been born.
I will move through the next period,
in and through this light!
I am unsure of myself and yet I also rejoice!
Pray now for my further development,
the development of us all and of our times.

Many who have died will become people of light
through your prayers.
After death, their own specific spiritual development continues.

If they are linked with Christ,
they will live and develop further in accord with creation.
They will live in and with creation.
They will live around the earth, near the earth.

*On the tenth of December of that same year, I saw Ramses II again.
He looked around and, wherever he looked, he saw light, much light.
I saw him later in a camel's stable. He leaned against the wall of the
high entrance for the camels. He looked into the dwelling place and
saw Mary, Joseph, the child Jesus, and a woman who was helping.
Ramses II looked for a long time at these people absorbing all within
himself. Then I saw how Ramses II, who was still standing at the
entrance, took a golden vessel in his arms, and said slowly:*

Creator of the universe and of the earth on which we live,
I ask that you fill this vessel with the light
that is in and around the child Jesus.
Let me bring this light to the people,
so that through it they find the link with you,
creator of heaven and earth!

*I saw the vessel being filled with light. Ramses II will pass it on to
humanity! He has experienced the birth of Christ. An angel spoke:*

Pray that the Chinese empress
also experiences the birth of Christ!
She too will pass on the light of Christ!

*The relative of mine, who had prayed for Ramses II in Egypt, ac-
companied me to the church on this day. While still in the church, I
gave her the words I had received to read. She asked me what Ramses
looked like. I described to her how I saw him in vision. She answered
that my description clearly resembled the mummy of Ramses that she
had seen in the Cairo museum.*

*The next day I saw in vision Ramses looking at Greece. His first task
was to bring the life of Christ to this land.*

*On the ninth of January 1998, I sat praying in the church and a saint
began to talk to me:*

The first three powerful thinkers and Greek men of spirit
to whom Ramses can pass on the life and light of creation
from praying to Christ are:
first Socrates, then Philip, and third Plato.
You are to pray for this too!
They will recognize the immensity of creation
and convey this to their people.
Only then will this spiritual power move over Europe
and large areas of India!
This is the beginning of a new spiritual awakening!

About ten days later, I saw that Ramses had grown in spirit. He absorbed much light within himself from the teachings of Jesus Christ. He was also in the process of learning the teachings of Paul and the history of the Apostles. On the fourth of March 1998, I saw in vision Ramses in Greece. He took the first steps toward India. Later that year he was moving toward the south of Russia. With much joy he said to me:

I bring greetings to friends there.
I will not go to the north of Russia.

The visions of Ramses II were immensely powerful and took a great deal of my energy. Slowly I began to realize what our prayers for the dead can do. Not only can they help the dead on their further journey through life in the next world, but, as Risen Ones, the dead can influence in positive ways, the future of humankind on earth. I regret that our church has not paid attention to this area of human experience. I know that the Catholic Church has taught that we should pray for the dead, but do Catholics fully realize what treasures are contained in these practices?

One Last Message

23.9.2000
The manuscript of this book was ready for publication. I went to the church to pray for all those people who are afraid of death. Suddenly St. Peter appeared to the left of the altar. To the right of the altar, I could see my risen son Peter, smiling. St. Peter spoke:

Listen!
I, Peter, ask you to follow me and listen to me now!
There is the creation of the human, there is Christ,
there is the period of the churches,
and now there follows a new spiritual period.
Humanity must know that the human is created by God
to exist in the resurrection of life.
Listen!
This magnificent, wonderful evolution of man and woman
is unique.
It is full of life, spiritual life.
I tell you now, as one risen from the dead:
the dynamics of the spiritual life of the individual human
are enormous.
Rejoice about this!
Don't forget you live on!
You will continue to live as the same individual, Joa!
All risen human beings remain their unique individual selves.
I can't tell you more, but I asked Christ
that I may convey this message to you and to all humankind.
Do not fear.
Peace and strength be with you all.
Amen.

Coda:
Let Us Give Thanks
and Praise to God

An angel once taught me how to pray:

Greet the day by receiving God's light:
We thank you, O Lord, for the sun, which rises in the morning,
for its light, which warms us.
Enlighten us, O Lord, with your light, which remains forever.
Amen.

Add to this prayer:
I lay before you the rotation of the earth.
Touch the earth's movements with your Spirit.
Shine through the earth so that it lives and dies not.

Stillness.

Clothe the earth with light and warmth,
so that growth of life is possible.
Touch the peoples of the earth—
the different races on different continents—
with light and spirit.
We ask you not to forsake humanity.
Let God's image and likeness unfold.
May we love the animals. Accept our blessing on them.
Open our eyes and our ears,
so that we recognize and absorb the entirety of creation.
Bless the water, the fire, and the storms.
May we live truthfully before you, O God.

Notes

Note to page 44.

Joa Bolendas believes that Teilhard de Chardin's understanding of man and the universe approximates more closely than any other to what she has received in visions. Teilhard attributes a spiritual and material aspect to all matter. "The time has come to realize that an interpretation of the universe—even a positivist one—remains unsatisfying unless it covers the interior as well as the exterior of things: mind as well as matter. The true physics is that which will, one day, achieve the inclusion of man in his wholeness in a coherent picture of the world."[1]

According to Teilhard, in its beginnings, the universe presents itself as an incredible organized whole. All matter is in a state of genesis. Elementary consciousness is already imprisoned in matter so that the increase both of spirit and of the complexity of matter is one and the same phenomenon. This upthrust of evolution continues through the biosphere, and only the postulation of an inner spiritual principle can explain the sharpness of direction that marks the process of irreversible advance to higher and more complex organisms. In human beings, evolution becomes conscious of itself. In the individual consciousness, an extension of one single organism over the entire earth takes place.

Finally, according to Teilhard, a further ascent of consciousness indicates the course of evolution toward an Omega point. Omega, another name for God, is the supreme fulfillment of the entire evolutionary process. Omega is the principle that explains love, which is understood as the inner affinity that unites beings with one another. It is also the principle that wards off the threat of disappearance, incompatible with reflective activity. For Teilhard, the overcoming of death is the irreversible thrust of

---

1. Teilhard de Chardin, *The Phenomenon of Man* (New York: Harper & Row, 1965), p. 35.

the whole evolutionary process. Through this process, all beings achieve their spiritualization and immortality as they move toward God. "When, in the universe in movement to which we have just awakened, we look at the temporal and spatial series diverging and amplifying themselves around and behind us like the laminae of a cone, we are perhaps engaging in pure science. But when we turn toward the summit, toward the totality and the future, we cannot help engaging in religion. Religion and science are the two conjugated faces or phases of one and the same complete act of knowledge—the only one which can embrace the past and future of evolution so as to contemplate, measure and fulfil them."[2]

Note to page 73.

Joa Bolendas asked Peter Barcaba to write a short introduction to help the reader better understand some of the difficult passages on the Austrian musician Franz Eibner. Peter Barcaba, himself a musician and former pupil of Franz Eibner, writes:

"What a privilege to follow step by step how the risen musician Franz Eibner discovers anew the wonder of music: the space of the keys (for example A, C, E as being complete) and within their overtones (from C to C1, in the octave) lies the full timbre of vibrations. He recognizes how the sound of a key (C) is preserved throughout all the progressions and transformations of a melody and manifests a point of God's light, which radiates throughout all creation. He recognizes the life and healing energy contained in vibrations.

"While alive on earth, Franz Eibner always presumed that diatonic (the seven stages of the major and minor scales, and all that developed in that way from ancient music) forms the foundation for all music that is truly great. The visions of Joa Bolendas reveal that there are seven vibrations in primordial existence (the vision has not been published in this book). Thus we may directly experience music as an image of God's creation. This is an overwhelming testimony that expresses our link with God through music!

---

2. Ibid., p. 285.

"According to the testimony of the risen Franz Eibner, the major and minor keys are an expression not only of basic musical experience but of primordial human values. They do not represent old traditions that can be changed but express perennial values never to be relinquished. For many hundreds of years, people recognized the character of certain tonalities. Eibner informs us about his new experiences in this area: B minor is a field of rest, the major key is a leaping stream. He also tells us about the evolution of music as corresponding to an increase of human consciousness. Sound, melody, sung speech, rhythm, and dance express an unfolding of music up to the overwhelming creations of the great musicians, in which the wealth of the vibrations find their highest artistic expression. Thus Eibner mentions certain composers, such as Bach, Schubert, Haydn, Chopin, Liszt, Ravel, and Mozart, not because of personal taste but because of the fulfilling and healing strength of their music.

"Finally, Eibner sees music as an energy that brings movement in human development—the powers of the soul begin to blossom, religious inspiration grows stronger. This momentous vision amazes Eibner, and us as well.

"We have received a great gift from heaven. Heaven is open and has permitted us to accompany Eibner and experience the wonderful development of a musician's spirit risen from the dead."

Harpist, singer, and composer **Therese Schroeder-Sheker** has maintained dual careers in music and in medicine. She made her Carnegie Hall debut in 1980, and has concertized as a soloist across eight countries and three continents. As a musician-clinician, she founded the palliative medical field of music-thanatology and the Chalice of Repose Project.

Educated in Dublin and at the Catholic University of America in Washington, D.C., **John Hill** is a Jungian analyst in private practice in Zurich, Switzerland. He is the author of numerous articles on Jungian themes and lectures at the C. G. Jung Institute in Zurich.